Ways into Literature

Ways into Literature

Stories, plays and poems
for pupils with SEN

Nicola Grove

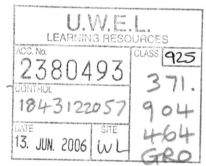
 David Fulton Publishers

David Fulton Publishers Ltd
The Chiswick Centre, 414 Chiswick High Road, London W4 5TF

www.fultonpublishers.co.uk

David Fulton Publishers is a division of Granada Learning Limited, part of ITV plc.

First published in Great Britain in 1998 by David Fulton Publishers as *Literature for All*
Second Edition 2005

British Library Cataloguing in Publication Data
A catalogue record for this book is available from the British Library.

ISBN 1-84312-205-7

10 9 8 7 6 5 4 3 2 1

Typeset by FiSH Books, London
Printed and bound in Great Britain

Contents

This book is dedicated to my grandfather, Percival Gurrey, Professor of English and Vice Principal of the University of the Gold Coast, whose teaching in the English Department at the Institute of Education inspired many of the people who taught me. The poetry he read to me as a child is everyone's inheritance.

Acknowledgements

This book is the outcome of work by many different people who have given me ideas and inspiration. In particular I would like to thank the following:

John Haynrych, head teacher of Kingsbury School, and Lynn Ranson, Advisory Teacher for Secondary English. Their enthusiastic support for literature in special schools has developed great expertise among teachers and support staff. Rosie Brown, Jane Grecic, Sue Lund and all the teachers who attended workshops generated a host of imaginative projects, some of which are described here.

My husband Bob, friends and colleagues Keith Park, Tina and Mike Detheridge, Julie Dockrell and Nick Peacey, who have consistently been prepared to drop everything and read drafts of the book whenever I demanded it. I have borrowed *Tongue Meat* from Keith Park's repertoire of stories.

Jane Miller, Ann Turvey, Tony Burgess, John Hardcastle and Anton Franks from the Institute of Education, London University, who provided time and space to discuss ideas on assessment and teaching. Olivia O'Sullivan from CLPE (Centre for Literacy in Primary Education) provided suggestions for the updating of Chapter 4 for this edition. Marie Gascoigne helpfully provided narratives by William Gascoigne-Brown.

Students from various places, including Mapledown School, Heathermount School, Kingsbury School, Sunfield and Ermine Road Day Centre, whose responses made me stop and think – and their teachers and key workers who were prepared to join in and take some risks. Isaac Sullivan from Sunfield for the inclusion of his great story *Wolves*.

Sarah Wimperis, of Graham-Cameron Illustration, for four drawings in Chapter 2.

The constructive, detailed feedback offered by Edwin Webb helped to clarify my ideas on emotion and perception. Peter Llewellyn-Jones provided valuable advice on translating texts into sign.

Material from the English National Curriculum is Crown Copyright, and is reproduced by kind permission of the Controller of HMSO.

An extract from Carolyn Fyfe's unpublished *Gulliver's Travels* (p. 45) is reproduced by kind permission of the author.

Figures 5.2–5.4, by Roderick Hunt, illustrated by Alex Brychta, from the Oxford Reading Tree, are reproduced by permission of Oxford University Press.

In Chapter 5, the stories and poems are reproduced with kind permission of the students and teachers who wrote them.

An extract from 'Red Boots On' (p. 50) is reprinted by kind permission of Kit Wright. 'Red Boots On' was originally printed in *The Bear Looked Over the Mountain*, Salamander Imprint.

An extract from 'What Has Happened to Lulu?' by Charles Causley (p. 103) is reprinted by kind permission of David Higham Associates.

'Overheard on a Saltmarsh' by H. H. Munro (p. 50), is reproduced by permission of Gerald Duckworth & Co. Ltd.

'Old Poem', translated from the Chinese by Arthur Waley (p. 104), copyright © The Arthur Waley Estate. Used by permission.

Extract from 'Tarantella' by Hilaire Belloc (p. 43) from *Complete Verse*, reprinted by permission of PFD on behalf of the estate of Hilaire Belloc. Copyright © 1970 Estate of Hilaire Belloc.

'Wind' by Ted Hughes (p. 54), copyright © The Estate of Ted Hughes/Faber and Faber.

'Breath' by Samuel Beckett (p. 14), copyright © Rosica Colin Ltd.

Extract from 'The Waking' by Theodore Roethke (p. 4). Copyright © 1942 Hearst Magazines Inc., published by Doubleday, a division of Random House Inc.

Every effort has been made to obtain permission to reproduce extracts from other authors' work. David Fulton Publishers will be happy to rectify any errors/omissions in any further edition.

Introduction

This book is a practical guide to using novels, plays and poetry with students across the full range of ability and with a particular focus on students with learning difficulties.

Because literature is the art of language, one of the key problems facing teachers is how to use age-appropriate texts with students whose ability to understand and use either written or spoken language is severely limited. *Ways into Literature* presents a structured framework for selecting and adapting texts, and describes a variety of rich and imaginative strategies designed by practising teachers for use in the classroom. It is for anyone who enjoys a good tale and wants to extend that experience to their students. The belief that underlies this book is that the best literature has a power which goes beyond words – and that literature is too important to be restricted to those who can read. This has implications for the ways in which literature is introduced to all students – but especially those with learning difficulties.

The advent of the National Curriculum opened up the teaching of a range of subjects for students with special educational needs. However, if we are to avoid token approaches to inclusion, we have to be prepared to address some of the subject-specific problems which accompany subject-specific opportunities. Within the English curriculum there are particular challenges in providing access to age-appropriate literature for students whose special needs are associated with difficulties in language and learning. These include:

- students with moderate, severe and profound learning difficulties;
- students with specific language and communication difficulties;
- students with hearing impairments;
- students whose difficulties fall within the autistic spectrum; and
- students with specific difficulties in reading and writing.

All of these students will find it hard to read and write about literary texts, but the underlying problem for all groups, except the last, is more fundamental than this: literature is the art of language, and delays or impairments to the understanding and use of spoken language will have a profound impact on the ability of such students to appreciate and respond to novels, plays and poetry. This is likely to be the case even if written texts are by-passed, and access is provided through storytelling and drama. Although there is an obvious appeal in the statement by the National Curriculum Council (1992) that: 'Students of different ages can respond to the same text in ways that are appropriate to their particular stage of development. What matters is how the invitation to respond is framed . . .', there is currently a real lack of explicit advice about how such 'framing' can best be done. It is still all too common to find that the only literature available to young people with learning difficulties is in the form of picture books designed for nursery children, and to observe a class of sixteen-year-olds listening to Eric Carle's *The Very Hungry Caterpillar*. I hasten to state at this point that we can all enjoy *The Very Hungry Caterpillar* from time to time. The problem occurs if this is the only kind of text teachers feel able to use with students who have learning difficulties.

This book focuses on creative ways of providing access to literature for all learners, regardless of their level of ability. Such a commitment forces us to confront some difficult issues which must be debated and resolved if the enjoyment of literature is to be a genuinely inclusive option within the curriculum and not a purely token one.

1 Literature in our lives

Literature may seem an irrelevance to many teachers working with students who have learning difficulties. The emphasis in the English curriculum for special educational needs has always been on the development of functional skills in communication and literacy – and it may be argued that 'doing Shakespeare' is a waste of time when a person cannot even 'cope with the basics'. Although stories are used extensively with younger children who have special educational needs, teachers seem to read or tell stories less frequently to older students. This may be partly because of the lack of age-appropriate resources, but perhaps storytelling and literature are also not seen as critical to the social and educational development of students with special needs. Stories tend to function something like sweets – an occasional treat rather than the basis of the diet.

This book is based on the belief that narrative and poetry are fundamental to our emotional and cognitive functioning, providing the means by which we make sense of our experiences and relate to those of others.

Suleiman and Rahila

These two young people were in their last year at school, and had fallen in love. Suleiman was a good-looking, streetwise young Muslim with quite severe difficulties in the understanding of language, masked by a superficial mastery of social conventions. Rahila was a Hindu girl with moderate learning difficulties, from a very over-protective and orthodox family. Suleiman had a place in a sheltered employment scheme, but Rahila was returning home for good. There was no chance at all of their even meeting or corresponding, let alone taking the relationship any further. As it happened, two teachers in the school were drama enthusiasts, and put on a production of *Romeo and Juliet*, *West Side Story*-style, with Suleiman and Rahila playing the leads. The events of the play dramatised their own situation with great poignancy.

> ## David
>
> David was attending a weekly group focusing on self-advocacy skills. He had strong views about some of the things that were going on in his day centre, including experiences of severe bullying. Unfortunately, his speech was extremely unintelligible, and was combined with a limited awareness of other people's reactions. He tended to hold forth in a monologue, and it was hard to respond to his concerns. On one occasion he was speaking at some length about an incident when I suddenly caught the word 'dagger'. My immediate reaction was horror – had the assaults changed from verbal to physical? I asked him to repeat what he had said. His actual words were, 'It was like a dagger in my heart.' David was using poetic language to express his feelings – but I had thought he must be describing a real attack, because I had not expected that a person with learning disabilities could use a figure of speech.

> The delighted recognition of ourselves in others and others in ourselves is one of the most potent insights literature can afford; and though younger children are not likely to register such moments in quite the same conscious way that older children or adults might, the possibility is nevertheless there for an increased awareness of the shared lineaments of our disparate natures.
>
> J. Fitzpatrick, in *Encouraging Expression: The Arts in the Primary Curriculum* by T. Roberts (ed.)

Language provides us with a means of communication, but too often we define this in terms of functional goals, such as requesting and labelling. But if, as many researchers now believe, the origins of language are in the sharing of experience, our starting points could be storytelling and conveying feelings. Literature is fundamentally concerned with the sharing of experience, and this is why it has been traditionally viewed as central to the English curriculum.

If students with special educational needs are to have access to a broad and balanced curriculum, provision of access to literature should be a primary concern for teachers. Our approach to teaching literature to students who may be neither able to read nor write, nor understand much of what is read to them, will be determined by the way we conceptualise the subject: as an aspect of literacy; an aspect of language; or a form of art.

The nature of literature

It is only in this century (and in the western hemisphere), that literacy has become widespread enough for us to assume that in order to experience or create 'literature' a person must be able to read and write. The groundlings at the Globe Theatre, the crowds who listened to the *Iliad* or *Beowulf*, or who gathered to watch *Oedipus Rex* or the York Mystery Plays, the audiences for the Mahabaratha in contemporary village India, or for *Sizwe Bansi is Dead* in Johannesburg in the 1970s, may not have been functionally literate, but they were capable of becoming engaged in works of literature. The earliest literature existed in oral form long before it was written down. Poetry, as well as drama, was originally a performance art, lyrics being the expression of personal emotion in song, epics and narratives being declaimed or sung like the border ballads of the sixteenth century.

Literature can be transmitted through a multitude of forms, which immediately opens up access for students who cannot read or write. It seems likely that far more people will ultimately access the classics through film, television and audio recordings than will ever read the originals. In fact, this principle was recognised in the Cox Report, which recommended that access to Shakespeare's plays be provided in a variety of media. We therefore need to define the term 'literacy' widely to include more than traditional print. Many students with special needs will also need alternative forms of communication and writing, such as manual signs or graphic symbols.

Literature is a part of the arts curriculum. The appeal of a poem or a story lies in its ability to excite the audience in a way which is first and foremost sensory. An encounter with the words evokes sensations and physiological responses, which generate affective states – of excitement, fear, contentment and loss. Our response is both emotional and intellectual. Our ability to evaluate a work of art is dependent on our ability to engage with it at a physical and an emotional level.

> A poem begins as a lump in the throat, a homesickness, a lovesickness. It finds the thought and the thought finds the word.
>
> (Robert Frost)
>
> Oh for a language of sensation rather than thought!
>
> (John Keats)

The purpose of arts education is emotional development through the creation of expressive forms (Ross 1978). This involves introducing students to works of art that will extend their imaginative experience, and teaching them to 'master the raw materials of self-expression in the arts'. The process begins with education of sensuous responses: 'help them to look and see, listen and hear, touch and feel, move and sense their own moving, encounter each other dramatically and be aware of each other's enacting'. Meanings are explored and created within the interaction with others, through the careful structuring and framing of experience provided by the nurturing adult.

Reading literature always involves a process of active creation of meaning in the encounter between the reader and the text. In developing access to literature as an aesthetic experience, we provide opportunities for individuals to experience and create meanings that are culturally significant within their particular contexts, as well as in the wider communities to which they belong.

Viewing feeling and sensation as the basis of response to literature changes how we think about the understanding of texts. Webb (1992) has used the terms 'apprehension' and 'comprehension'. Apprehension is our immediate sensory appreciation of the text, even if we cannot fully comprehend its meaning. This insight is remarkably compatible with recent views on the nature of linguistic comprehension and expression, which are described in more detail in Chapter 2.

> Affection! thy intention stabs the centre
> With what's unreal thou coactive art,
> And fellowst nothing; then 'tis very credent
> Thou may'st conjoin with something; and thou dost
> And that beyond commission, and I find it,
> And that to the infection of my brains
> And hard'ning of my brows.
>
> (Shakespeare, *A Winter's Tale*, Act I, Sc. 2)

> The precise meaning of this powerful text is difficult to decode. However, we sense the onslaught of the character's tormented logic, through a process of sensory apprehension.

CHAPTER 2 Language, emotions and response to literature

I see it feelingly.

(Shakespeare, *King Lear*, Act IV, Sc. 6)

We think by feeling. What is there to know?
I hear my being dance from ear to ear.
I wake to sleep, and take my waking slow.

(Theodore Roethke, 'The Waking')

This chapter explores the relationship between language, feelings and response to literature. Because literature is the art of language, it is important to understand how language develops in children. This will allow us to identify some starting points for using stories and poems with pupils whose language is delayed. It seems common sense to assume that children will only be able to benefit from a text if they can fully understand the language in it. The trouble is that this approach means that we would never move beyond simple nursery rhymes and picture stories for pupils with significant learning difficulties, where language may not have progressed much beyond 'infant' levels. In fact, when we look at theories of language development and theories about response to works of art, the situation is much more fluid and ambiguous than this.

Language development

'Gladly my cross I'd bear' – a hymn – was often understood as 'Gladly, my cross-eyed bear'.

There are two aspects to language: comprehension (understanding what others say) and production (talking or communicating to others). Understanding or comprehension involves a process of recognising speech sounds and matching them to meaning. Sometimes this results in errors or ambiguity – for example, when a word has one pronunciation but different meanings.

Production, or expression, involves the ability to put thoughts into words and communicate them to others. These two aspects of language are complementary and develop alongside each other. In both, the brain acts as a processor of information.

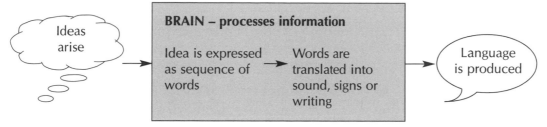

Figure 2.1

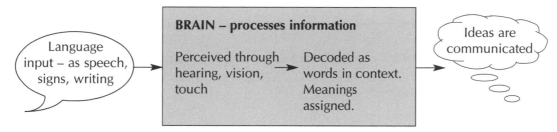

Figure 2.2

The traditional view of language development is that a child starts by understanding and producing individual words and then goes on to phrases with two or three words, eventually progressing to complex sentence structures. This hierarchical model is the basis of many influential assessment and intervention programmes, for example the Derbyshire Language Scheme (Knowles and Masidlover 1982) or Living Language (Locke 1985).

However, a study by Nelson in 1973 showed that some children express themselves early on in whole phrases, as well as in single words. It now seems that children learn to comprehend language in a similar way. Knowledge of how language develops is important when we are thinking about access to literature.

Comprehension

During the earliest period of language development, infants pick up cues from vocal tone and stress. They develop understanding of words and phrases through their experience, by associations with familiar routines and events. By three months, infants will respond empathetically when they hear another baby crying. Young children rely more on contextual cues, stress and intonation than on the words and sentence structure. They become familiar with structures used in different contexts, for example instructions and greetings, and with the tone of voice and non-verbal language associated with different emotions. This familiarity with structural frameworks helps to build comprehension (Bloom 1993).

> We understand stories not by adding up the parts, but by bringing to our perception of stories a mental model of how stories work.
>
> (Fox 1993)

Amrita (three months) is soothed by her mother singing a familiar song.

Hester (six months) laughs ecstatically when her French cousin says in a teasing voice over and over again 'Tu suces ta pouce' ('You're sucking your thumb').

Joe (nine months) looks at his feet when his mum says, 'Where are your SHOES?' and stops what he is doing when she says 'NO' firmly.

Gideon (12 months) picks up the phone and puts it to his ear.

Young children use familiar contexts, tone of voice and routines to make sense of what they hear. In fact, we go on doing this all our lives. It is not enough to 'decode' sequences of words to retrieve meaning, because there is always a gap between what the speaker intends and what the listener understands. This gap is filled by inference. We make active guesses and predictions that help us to understand, and we enrich literal meanings from our own experience and our perception of the setting.

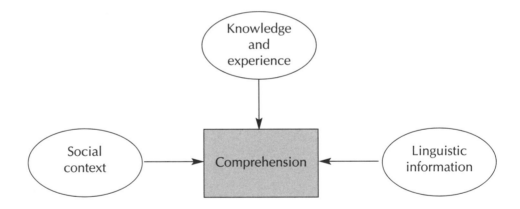

Figure 2.3 Research shows that knowledge and experience of the world, social context and linguistic information interact dynamically in comprehension (Sperber and Wilson 1986)

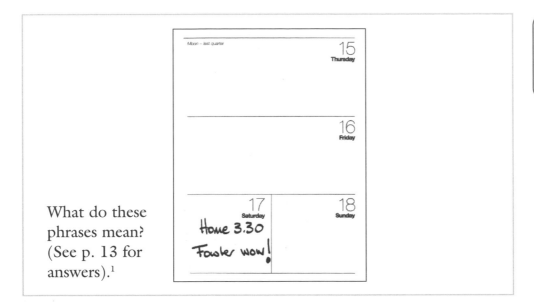

What do these phrases mean? (See p. 13 for answers).[1]

> We can decode this linguistically, but it makes no sense unless we have other information about the context.

Complete this sentence:

If I left you ...[2]

> This example illustrates that in real-life conversation we draw on our existing knowledge and mentally complete sentences by anticipating their meaning. For suggested meanings, see p. 13.

If you have a patched system, it's very unlikely that your PC has DSO exploit. However, there is a bug in Spybot, which means it can find this exploit repeatedly and apparently fail to fix it.[3]

> In this example, unless you know what the topic is, you will find it hard to work out the meaning, even though you can comprehend the basic sentence construction.

Expression

Experience and knowledge of context are equally important in developing expressive language. Although language is inventive, much of what we communicate is relatively predictable in certain contexts. We associate events with particular 'scripts' – the behaviour patterns, both verbal and non-verbal, that we are likely to use in any given situation. Routine phrases such as 'Happy birthday', 'How are you?' and 'up and down' seem to be acquired as whole units rather than as separate words. Young children's knowledge of scripts and routines helps them to associate language and events, and to use language appropriately. Scripts and routines gain meaning from the association between an event and the emotions that arise – pleasurable or painful, humorous or sad. Emotions are the earliest and most fundamental impulse for communication.

Examples of routine phrases learned as whole units:

See you later.
Peep-bo.
Oh no!
Up you come!
Where's it GONE?

And in adulthood:

From media and TV:

Points mean prizes.
You are the weakest link.

Routine instructions:
Mind the gap.
The person you are calling is not available. Please leave a message after the tone.

Many social phrases function in this way:
Excuse me.
Can't be helped.
Have a nice day.
Oh, well.
No way!
You hear what I'm saying?
I'm cool with that.

As do idioms:
Can of worms.
Made to measure.
If the cap fits . . .
Happy as a sandboy.

Children also enjoy language as a form of play from a very early age, manipulating sounds, rhythms and tones of voice. For example, children babble to themselves and rehearse sounds and sayings they have heard during the day (Weir 1962). The researcher David Crystal has suggested that when a child with severe learning difficulties enjoys the dramatic contrasts of tones in a game of 'Peep-bo', this is on a continuum with the 'cerebral bliss' experienced by a reader of James Joyce's *Finnegan's Wake*.

KEY POINTS:

- In understanding language, context, familiarity, rhythm and tones of voice are as important as the actual words used. So we can make use of these features when we read stories and poetry with children.

- In using language, quite complex sequences can be learned and used as whole units without necessarily understanding every word. We can emphasise parts of a text that children can repeat and learn by heart without worrying too much about how complex the language is.

Emotional development

The English National Curriculum lays much emphasis on children's ability to analyse critically literature and language, but much less on enjoyment or emotional response to literature. This is unfortunate, not just for pupils with special needs, but for all children, because the emotions play a very large part in determining how we respond to works of art and how we learn to understand and appreciate them.

Brain research

Research into the neurophysiology of emotion has shown that emotional responses are located in the amygdala-limbic structures situated above the brainstem. Individuals who have lost their amygdala through surgery or trauma do not experience emotional response. There is evidence that the amygdala acts independently of the cortex, or 'thinking' brain, suggesting that feeling is the precursor of thought, rather than the other way round. This independence between 'emotion' and 'thought' also suggests that emotional impressions and memories can be evoked even in people whose cognition is impaired or severely delayed.

'The fact that the thinking brain grew from the emotional reveals much about the relationship of thought to feeling: there was an emotional brain long before there was a thinking one.'

(From D. Goleman, *Emotional Intelligence*)

Since literature demands emotional engagement, we need to understand something about affective development and how emotion and thought interrelate. We are born with the means to express both positive and negative emotions, and the earliest signals of distress and delight, interest, fear, anger and surprise emerge by about three months. By about the

A core of primary emotions that are recognisable across cultures:

> anger
> sadness
> fear
> enjoyment
> love
> surprise
> disgust
> shame

age of five months, babies distinguish happy, sad and angry vocalisations, particularly with the additional cue of facial expression (Bloom 1993).

The purpose of language is, above all, expressive – to give form to states of mind and feeling. Children convey feelings through non-verbal behaviour, until they have developed the vocabulary and cognitive ability to talk explicitly about feelings. This close tie-up between language and feeling is the basis of literature, and of poetic language such as metaphor. Stripped of emotion, stories lose their power. It is only through feeling and personal involvement that a story becomes a story rather than a list of events.

The following is an example of a traditional story, where the words that convey feelings have been edited out. Note that these are not only the adjectives, but also descriptive and emotive verbs such as 'screamed'; the sinister form of address traditionally used by the wolf, 'My dear' and the rhetorical language that helps build up suspense and at the same time gives a sense of control, 'What big eyes you have/All the better to see you with'. These aspects are what Labov and Waletzky (1967) call 'evaluations'. They let the reader/listener know what attitude they should be adopting to the people and events in the story.

Red Riding Hood was told by her mother to take a basket of food to her grandmother, and not to stop on the way. As she went through the woods she met a wolf. The wolf asked her where she was going. Red Riding Hood said she was going to visit her grandmother. The wolf said he would go too. He went to the grandmother's house and knocked on the door. When he came in he ate the grandmother and dressed in her clothes.

Red Riding Hood knocked on the door, and the wolf said 'Come in.' Red Riding Hood came to the bed and looked at the wolf. She said, 'You have big eyes.'

'That's so I can see you,' said the wolf.

'You have big ears,' said Red Riding Hood.

'That's so I can hear you,' said the wolf.

'You have big teeth,' she said.

'That's so I can eat you,' said the wolf.

Red Riding Hood ran out of the door and called for help. A woodcutter came and killed the wolf. When he cut open its stomach, the grandmother came out. He ate the cakes Red Riding Hood had brought.

Red Riding Hood went home.

You might like to try reading this aloud in a very bland, unemotional way, then rewrite it including all the features that make the story exciting and funny, and read it again with feeling.

KEY POINT:

- When using literature with pupils, we need to aim for emotional engagement, by emphasising the way the story or poem makes us feel – not necessarily by talking about this, but in the way we present it. Once children are emotionally engaged they will be attentive, and once they attend, they can begin to understand and remember.

How we respond to literature

Having considered how language and emotions develop, let us think about what actually happens when we first encounter a story or a poem. Webb (1992) argues that our response to literature, or any other form of art, begins not with analysis but with a sensory experience (seeing, hearing, touching) that gives rise to a feeling which, in turn, leads us to develop an attitude or a conscious response.

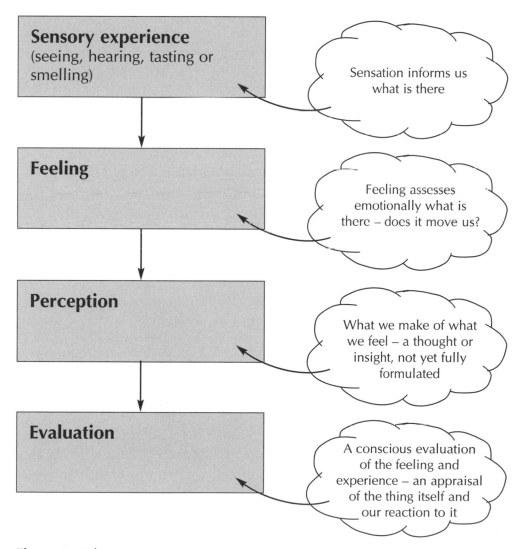

Figure 2.4 The response to art

Figure 2.4 shows that there is a starting point (in sensation) that is accessible to everyone. The key to sharing literature with students who have learning difficulties is to develop their responses as far along the process as possible, without excluding pupils who may never be able to talk about or analyse a text, but who have the capacity for sensation and emotional feelings.

Implications for teaching

Feelings and emotions are key to the development of communication and the ability to comprehend the mental states of other people, and are the ground of response to literature as an art form. By placing emotional response at the centre of our work, we may be able to find ways of reaching students whose intellectual difficulties preclude the development of advanced skills in literacy and decoding.

This means that we can take several routes to adapting texts. We do not have to be limited by students' linguistic comprehension of a story or poem: we can work through feelings and sensory perception. We can simplify the language by adapting it to the level of the individual – telling stories in simple, short sentences, or even sequences of single words. Here we start with the child's level of understanding. At the same time, we can enrich the text by creating sensory associations through tone of voice and visual and sound effects that add contextual meaning. Some units of text can be presented as complete scripts and treated like stretches of atmospheric music. Here the starting point is the text. Figure 2.5 summarises these two approaches.

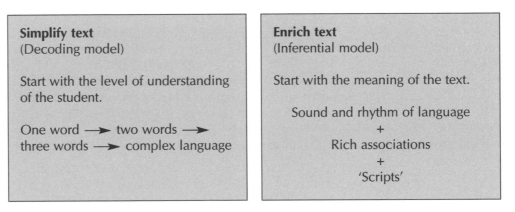

Figure 2.5 Two approaches to meaning

In the next chapter we look at the structure of stories, plays and poetry, and ways of adapting them for students who have difficulties in language and learning.

Answers to comprehension problems on page 7

1. Note left by my 16-year old daughter who had been out to a party the night Robbie Fowler scored a hat trick for Liverpool FC.
2. Said by my husband one evening as he emptied his pockets. By the time he had completed the sentence ('...£5 for tomorrow, would that be enough till you can get to the bank?') I had already run through my mind the issues of who would deal with the car, and what days he would be able to have the children.
3. 'Inside IT', *Guardian*, 8 July 2004 – reply to query).

1. Note left by my 16-year old daughter who had been out to a party the night Robbie Fowler scored a hat trick for Liverpool FC.
2. Said by my husband one evening as he emptied his pockets. By the time he had completed the sentence ('...£5 for tomorrow, would that be enough till you can get to the bank?')

3 Adapting stories, plays and poetry

I'll tell you a story
About Jackanory
And now my story's begun.
I'll tell you another
About John his brother
And now my story is done.

(Traditional)

Faint brief cry and immediately inspiration and slow increase of light *together* reaching maximum *together* in about ten seconds. Silence and hold about five seconds.

Expiration and slow decrease of light together reaching minimum together...in about ten seconds and immediately cry as before. Silence and hold about five seconds.

(Samuel Beckett, *Breath*)

Principles of adaptation

To adapt a text for presentation you need to consider the nature of the text, the purpose of the presentation, the audience and the methods of presentation you will use. These stages can be summarised as What? Why? Who? and How? (see table opposite)

Structural frameworks – looking at texts

A work of literature only comes alive in the mind of its audience, who understand its meaning by filtering it through their individual life experiences. In this sense, every text is realised in a thousand different ways. My *Romeo and Juliet* will not be quite the same as yours. Sharing stories, plays or poems with an audience always involves an interpretation. When aspects of the original are changed or selectively heightened, the interpretation becomes an adaptation. In adapting texts, we need to know what we are changing, and why we are doing it.

What?	■ Any text that excites you enough to want to share it.
	■ Any text that interests the students.
Why?	■ The aim is for students to have some knowledge of the best stories, plays and poetry around, reflecting a variety of cultures and styles.
	■ To develop students' imagination, empathy, engagement, self-expression and shared knowledge of texts.
Who?	■ All students can benefit from exposure to good stories and poetry – but you need to take their individual strengths and needs into consideration when planning.
	■ The guiding principle is 'partial participation' – students should be given the opportunity to take part in experiences at whatever level is appropriate for them.
How?	■ Performance, music and pictorial illustrations can be amplified with other sensory associations – smells, tastes and tactile stimuli.
	■ Alternative forms of communication and writing, for example signing and using symbols.
	■ We can enable students to experience something of the essence of a text, even if they cannot grasp everything. Students who cannot decode all the language may still get a sense of the meaning through repeated associations and inference.
	■ It is vitally important to give students enough time to become familiar with the work, through repetition. Often it is only after about the third or fourth time that you present a story or poem that you will see any response. Do not fall into the trap of thinking that you must do something new every lesson – regardless of what visiting inspectors may try to tell you!

When you tell someone that you have just read a new novel, one of the first questions they are likely to ask is: 'What's it about?' In your answer you will probably say something about the type of book (for example a crime story or a romance), its main message, something about the plot, something about the people in the book and something about its atmosphere. You might also mention the style of the writing, if it is sufficiently striking to you. These are the basic elements of literature, and in any particular text some may be more prominent than others. In many thrillers, for example, plot is emphasised at the expense of character. Analysing how these elements combine in a particular text is a good starting point for an adaptation.

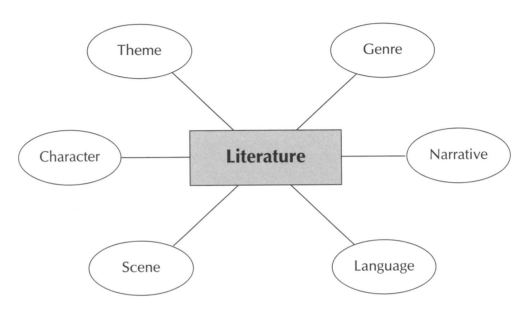

Figure 3.1 The basic elements of literature

Theme

The central issue that the author wishes to convey. There may be more than one theme, and particular chapters, verses or scenes may have their own themes.

Deciding what is the main theme allows you to anchor the presentation of the text.

Genre

This is the style of writing, and is related to the theme. Examples include thrillers, romance, horror, detective fiction, tragedy and comedy. Each genre has associated traditions, which set up expectations in the minds of the audience or readers.

Some texts do not conform to any particular genre, but identifying conventions can help to establish the atmosphere and tone of how you present the text. For example, there are typical kinds of music associated with chase, murder, knockabout comedy and love, which you can use to bring a sense of coherence to activities.

Deciding on theme and genre is a good starting point for working on a text. If you know the theme you wish to get across, you can start to select and combine other elements of the text to convey this.

Plot

The plot or story line is the path along which the work travels. At its most basic, a story line involves an event with a start point and an end point, as the 'Jackanory' rhyme suggests. Beckett's *Breath* suggests that the start and the end are all that is important – and these are universal. Narrative is driven by action and consequence, which link the event to character through motive.

Some students may not be able to follow a plot, but will be sensitive to the signals that open and close events in their daily lives. You can exploit this awareness in symbolic form in your presentation of narratives.

For students with special educational needs, the best narratives are usually those with a strong, explicit and logical story line that can be simplified without too much omission or distortion of the original.

Character

The imaginary people in a story are brought to life by the author's ability to create impressions that are vivid and real, and our feelings and responses to the plot. Exploring character involves analysing their motives and actions in the events of the story, what they say, and how they are described.

A sense of character can be gained by quite small characteristics. The actress Dame Peggy Ashcroft used to say that she always started with the shoes when building up her characters for the stage. In a workshop for teachers, we had a lot of fun planning how to portray one of Thomas Hardy's characters through smell. (For those who know *Far From the Madding Crowd* – what aftershave would you say Sergeant Troy wore?)

For students with special educational needs, the best characters are usually those who can be easily identified and contrasted, who lend themselves to role-play, and whose feelings and motives can be readily deduced from their actions. For example, characters whose speech patterns and actions are highly distinctive, or characters who are described in very visual terms.

Scene

This is the context in which the action takes place. It also sets its atmospheric tone. By exploring the scene, you create the backdrop for the plot and characters. Explicit information about scene is provided by the stage directions in a play, or descriptions of setting in a novel.

Developing atmosphere offers enormous potential for conveying something of the essence of a text to people who have difficulties understanding language.

For students with special educational needs, look for strongly atmospheric and contrastive scenes, which lend themselves to illustration through sensory effects – art, colour, music and sounds, textures, smells.

Language

The language of poetry, plays and novels presents the biggest stumbling block for students who have learning difficulties – but once the language is changed, we are in danger of losing the core of the work. You can retell and simplify the story of a Shakespeare play, but if you use none of the original text, are you offering students anything of any value?

Following the principle of partial participation you may not be able to use the whole text, but you should be able to use extracts. Even the most complex texts will have some passages that are written simply enough to be used directly. Accessible language styles have the following characteristics:

- *Simplicity*

  Simple sentence construction and basic vocabulary. As a test, can you easily sign it or translate it into graphic symbols?

- *Concreteness*

  Descriptive language referring to sensory experiences, which can be illustrated by real examples or pictures. For example 'Plump, unchecked cherries . . . bloom-down-cheeked peaches', from 'Goblin Market' by Christina Rossetti.

- *Rhythm and sound*

  Language that is strongly patterned and conveys meaning through both sound and sense. 'Onomatopoeia' is the technical term for words with in-built sound effects (for example moo, splat, tee-hee, pitter-patter). It can be illustrated with sounds or music, using contrasts between vowels and consonants; short sounds and long sounds; hard sounds and soft sounds. For people with profound and complex needs, or dual sensory impairments, it is very effective if they lie on a resonance board (see panel) and feel the rhythm tapped and called around them.

- *Repetition*

  Language that builds up meaning through repeated sequences and refrains (for example, traditional folk and fairy tales, songs and ballads).

- *Dramatic language*

  Language that conveys character, or narrative, and can be illustrated through acting, exaggerated for emphasis.

Appendix 1 provides some examples of poetry that use these different aspects of language.

Making a resonance board
Use a single piece of plywood roughly 120 cm square, 6–8 mm thick, stanging on a 2.5 cm rim. Highly polished wood carries the sound best. For larger pupils, put two boards together.

Choosing texts

You can use the planning framework on p. 20 to identify the main elements of a text, in order to decide what elements you will focus on and whether the text is a suitable choice for a particular group of students.

The basic elements – theme, genre, narrative, character, scene and language – are not always present in equal measure. For example, take this poem by Thomas Wyatt:

> I promised you
> And you promised me
> To be as true
> As I would be.
> But since I see
> Your double heart
> Farewell my part!

Lyrics like this are designed to express directly the feelings of the poet. There is no narrative, nor character. The components are language and mood (the internalised 'scene' or context).

Dickens' *Pickwick Papers* has a very vivid cast of characters, exuberant language and a clearly defined scene, but far less emphasis on narrative. By contrast, a thriller such as *Day of the Jackal* offers an engrossing narrative, but little character interest.

Other criteria to consider

When you are choosing a novel, play or poem to use with students, you should also consider:

- *Cultural significance to individuals or communities*

  Works that have had a lasting influence on the development of literature.

  Images, events and characters that have popular recognition and lead to shared experiences. For example, the Mahabaratha is the most well-known epic in India and is reinforced through endless TV, comic and film versions.

  Familiar extracts and clichés are often indications that a work has cultural significance. Even if your pupils only grasp one line, knowing 'Romeo, Romeo, wherefore art thou Romeo?' gives them a toehold in the wider community. Catchphrases are likely to be reinforced in future, even if only through advertisements.

  Works that are relevant to students' current experience. For example, stories related to class visits, emotional needs of students, life transitions such as leaving school.

Choosing a text – planning a basic approach

Theme and genre

- What is the main point or theme of the text?
- Is it in a particular genre, for example, heroic epic, thriller, romance, comedy, tragedy.
- Does the genre suggest any musical or other conventions?

Plot

- Summarise the main story line
- Ideas for conveying the story line to students.
- What are the main events?
- Ideas for conveying the main events to students

Character

- Who are the main characters?
- Who are the minor characters?
- Which characters will you include?
- Ideas for conveying the characters to students

Scene

- What scenes or moods provide the setting for the main events?
- Ideas for conveying the atmosphere to students.

Language

Choose some extracts from the text that are:

- in simple, direct language that some of your students could understand;
- in evocative, descriptive language that could be enriched with sensory association;
- in rhythmic, patterned language that you could move to, or use like a piece of music;
- very well known;
- important to story line or character.

Primary focus

What will your primary focus be in your adaptation?

- Narrative
- Character
- Scene
- Language

- *Film and TV versions*

  It is an advantage if the text you want to use is available on video. Beware of simplified animated versions – although these can be useful as summaries of the story, they may not hold pupils' attention. If you are exploring feelings, motives and reactions, real actors are much better, although you may have to be selective and use extracts, filling in the story line yourself.

- *Your favourites!*

  This is the most important principle of all. If you love a text, you will find a way to share it.

Adapting language – simplification and enrichment

In the previous chapter it was suggested that two approaches to conveying meaning can operate in parallel: simplification and enrichment.

Simplification

This approach starts with the child. The principle involves providing input at a level appropriate to the child's ability to decode language, simplifying or explaining vocabulary, and making few assumptions about what the child may be using from the context. Using the terminology of the *Derbyshire Language Scheme* (Knowles and Masidlover 1982), we build up from one 'information carrying' word, to two words, to three words, to four words, and thence to 'grammar and complex language'.

As soon as we look at a complex text, it becomes apparent that this approach will be inadequate if we want to provide children with real experiences of literature. For example, consider this speech from Macbeth.

	Now o'er the one half world
50	Nature seems dead, and wicked dreams abuse
51	The curtain'd sleep. Witchcraft celebrates
52	Pale Hecate's offerings, and withered murder
53	Alarumed by his sentinel, the wolf,
54	Whose howl's his watch, thus with his stealthy pace
55	With Tarquin's ravishing strides, towards his design
56	Moves like a ghost. Thou sure and firm-set earth
57	Hear not my steps, which way they walk, for fear
58	The very stones prate of my whereabouts
59	And take the present horror from the time
60	Which now suits with it. Whiles I threat, he lives
61	Words to the heat of deeds too cold breath gives.

Shakespeare, *Macbeth*, Act II, Sc. 1: 49–61)

On the face of it, this passage is fraught with difficulty if you want to use it with students who have difficulties in language and learning. The syntax is complex (try to sort out what all the different 'his'es refer to in lines 53–5, or the subjects of the verbs in lines 58–9). There are numerous impenetrable classical allusions. The language is archaic and worse, when we do recognise a word (such as 'watch', 'present', 'suits') the meaning is likely to be quite other than that which first occurs to us. If we try to paraphrase the speech, we come up with something so banal, we wish we had never started:

Macbeth speech – simplified version

It is night and everything is quiet. Witches, wolves and ghosts prowl around . . . Earth – do not listen to my steps. While I stand here talking, he goes on living. The more I talk, the more my desire to act grows cold . . .

Enrichment

Here we start with the text and explore its atmosphere, meaning and sound. Instead of decoding it into a simpler version, we consider the sub-text, the context, and the impact of allusions, and translate these into sensory associations that illustrate and embody the feeling in which the text is grounded. We use the sound and rhythm of language, and whole phrases, which function as 'scripts' associated with particular events. This 'top-down' approach actively exploits context to create experiences and bring the text to the child.

In the case of the *Macbeth* speech, we might ask the following questions:

● *How does the sound of the text relate to its meaning?*

If you read the text aloud, and try moving to its rhythms, you will see how much of it is written in half lines. The sense trips over from one line to the next, in a way that mirrors Macbeth's fearful, jerky thoughts. If we take 'Hear not my steps' as the basis for working with the text, we can move first in one direction, then another, then stop, then start again (you can push a wheelchair to this rhythm). Although there are only four sentences, it is difficult to read the speech aloud with only four pauses. If we take our breaths at the commas, after each phrase, we immediately get a sense of gasping panic. We have now got a long way into feeling what the passage tells us, without any decoding at all.

● *What images and associations are called up by the text?*

The images are associated with darkness and death (the 'cold breath' of line 61 is a dramatic irony). So we might darken the room, creating a shadow on a backcloth with light or torch, and introduce the occasional scary noise (a wolf howl, the sounds of our steps).

● *Which parts of the text work as whole scripts?*

After reading the whole speech to the students and encouraging them to move and vocalise through it, you could separate sections to be programmed onto speech output devices, activated by switches. Macbeth shifts the psychological perspective from external to internal in this speech; first he is the observer of the night, then a partner in a dialogue, then he reflects on himself and his actions. Each perspective can be taken by a different student.

Enriching texts does not preclude simplifying them. Once students have made the emotional connections with the speech, it is possible to go back to it, translate, and help them to decode meanings. The difference is, though, that you are giving them the whole experience and adding in the simpler meanings – not stripping the text of its resonance, and leaving them with the bare bones of the paraphrase.

For this reason, it is vital to go back to the original text for your inspiration, rather than relying on simplified versions, which do not have the rich symbolic significance which you will need to adapt. For example, if you work from a story version of *Romeo and Juliet*, you will miss the hand-to-hand contact described in the sonnet of their first exchange, which would allow you to dramatise the relationship in a relevant tactile way for pupils with sensory impairments.

In a workshop on *Far from the Madding Crowd*, one teacher realised that although the film uses a wide open space as the context for Troy's seduction of Bathsheba, the original location is enclosed and secret. This provided a starting point for thinking about how to create the right atmosphere for the scene with pupils who have profound learning difficulties.

Applying the framework: *Far from the Madding Crowd*

Thomas Hardy is one of the authors recommended for study at Key Stage 3, and *Far from the Madding Crowd* is one of his most accessible books. It is highly atmospheric, set in rural Dorset through changing seasons and with many references to contemporary folk songs and dances, which can be used to provide musical illustrations. The characters and the story line can be simplified without too much distortion.

Theme and genre

The themes of love and loss are archetypal in their appeal.
The genre is essentially romantic fiction.

Plot

Summary of main story line

Gabriel Oak is a shepherd who loves the beautiful but headstrong Bathsheba Everdene. When he loses all his flock in an accident, he goes to work for her at her farm. Bathsheba is courted by her rich neighbour, Farmer Boldwood, but she falls for Sergeant Troy, a handsome ne'er-do-well, and marries him. Troy has already seduced her maid, Fanny, who dies in childbirth. He disappears, but re-enters Bathsheba's life just as she is about to marry Boldwood. Boldwood shoots Troy and goes to prison, and Bathsheba realises that, after all, Gabriel is the man for her.

Main events

Troy seduces Bathsheba.
The storm.

Characters

Gabriel: strong, patient, trustworthy.
Bathsheba: beautiful, proud.
Troy: handsome, faithless, greedy.
Boldwood: silent, serious, rich.
Fanny: sad, poor.

Troy seduces Bathsheba

Troy and Bathsheba meet in an enclosed green dell, where he entertains her with a display of sword drill. Bathsheba stands firm as his sword flashes around her – 'Don't you trust me not to hurt you?' he asks. Of course, we know that Troy is actually a bounder and a cad, who is after her money, and will break her heart. At the end of the scene, they embrace.

The main emphasis in this episode is on atmosphere and character relationships rather than narrative, although when we are tracing the overall story line, this scene is pivotal.

Themes:

Trust and betrayal.
Passion.

Characters:

Bathsheba (white, flower scent: innocence, beauty).
Troy (red, tacky aftershave, gold chains on hairy chest: army, danger, passion).

Scene:

A green, enclosed, quiet space. Use dappled or green lighting, birdsong, gentle wind as the background.

Activities:

Sword drill: Using light beams, torches or silver foil swords, the students take it in turns to act Troy and Bathsheba in the centre of a circle.
The kiss: Use red and white streamers intertwined to link Troy and Bathsheba together. This is an echo of the way Troy winds a lock of her hair around his finger as a keepsake.
Language: Extracts from the dialogue: 'Stand still'; 'Are you sure you won't hurt me?'; 'Quite sure'; 'One, two, three, four'; 'Is the sword sharp?'; 'Oh no!'; 'I must be leaving you'.
Trust: Enact the theme of betrayal by playing tricks. For example, the game where a person is shown obstacles around the room, then blindfolded and led around the course – but in the meantime, all the obstacles have been removed. The partner is actually tricking them and betraying their trust.

The storm

On Troy and Bathsheba's wedding night, there is a dance for all the farmhands. Troy gets the men drunk, and refuses to come out when Gabriel warns him that there will be a storm, and that they should cover the hay ricks. The emphasis here is more on the narrative – the conflict.

Themes:

Conflict; storm.

Narrative:

Gabriel pleads with Troy and his friends to come out and help him. They refuse.

Characters:

Gabriel (wants to work). Troy (wants to play).

Scene:

Contrast between indoors (the barn) which is safe and warm and full of light, laughter and dance music, with the outside, dark and wet and dangerous, with storm noises.

Activities:

Conflict: Dramatise this with a tug-of-war. Start with Troy and Gabriel on opposite ends. Other students join in on one or other side, using lines from the episode such as: 'Protect the ricks/hay'; 'It will not rain'; 'A heavy rain will fall'; 'We'll enjoy ourselves'.
At the end of the tug-of-war, Troy's followers win, and they fall back on the floor in a 'drunken stupor'.
The storm: Use musical instruments, tapping on backs or drumming on the floor, water sprays, to build up the storm. At its height, there should be thunder, lightning and driving rain.

Build a 'rick' with chairs and wedges. Two pupils try to cover it with a large sheet, while being blown on and rained on by the storm.

Language:

Dialogue from the scene (as above). Phrases that refer to the storm, for example: 'The lightning was the colour of silver, and gleamed in the heavens'; 'Rumbles became rattles'; 'All was silent, and black as a cave'; 'From every part of the tumbling sky there came a shout'.

Scene:

Contrast between indoors (the barn) which is safe and warm and full of light, laughter and dance music, with the outside, dark and wet and dangerous, with storm noises.

Responding to literature

Looking overall at the process of response described in Chapter 2, from sensation to feeling to perception to cognitive evaluation – let us see how it applies to the work we do with literature.

Sensation ⟶ Feeling ⟶ Perception ⟶ Evaluation

Figure 3.2 The response continuum

First, we create *sensation* through the way we present the work – both directly through saying the text out loud; and treating it like music and through multisensory illustration – what we choose for the scene and characters.

Then we aim for emotional engagement – the *feeling* stage, by emphasising the mood and atmosphere, and the effect inherent in the language.

This leads to selective attention and *perception* by students, who will demonstrate a range of ways of engaging – for some they may be looking at or feeling props; others will recall and echo snatches of text that appeal to them.

Only when students have become familiar in this way with the text is it productive to move to the fourth stage – *cognitive/analytic response* and discussion, with those who have the verbal abilities to express opinions and judgements.

KEY POINTS:

This chapter presents a framework for working with texts that are age-appropriate, and involve complex language and plots. The basic principles are:

- Choose stories and poems that you love yourself.
- Use the original text in your planning.
- Enrich the meaning through multisensory illustration.
- Aim to help students engage emotionally with the text, by heightening the feelings through the way you read it, musical accompaniment (this is the third stage of response: feeling).
- Explain as you go, but keep a balance between explanation and experience.
- When the students are very familiar with the text, you can talk about it with them and encourage them to analyse aspects of it.

CHAPTER 4 Literature in the classroom: from principles to practice

Philosophies and principles offer starting points, but translating these into practice in the classroom can seem a daunting task. The sheer diversity of difficulties in language and communication means that approaches that work brilliantly with some students will fall totally flat with others. Teachers need to become 'magicians', weaving different spells from the same ingredients to open different doors to the world of imagination.

This chapter begins with tried and tested approaches from drama and English teaching for enabling students to engage with texts. The next section identifies some of the particular difficulties in language and learning for students with moderate/severe learning difficulties, autism, specific language impairment, deafness and profound and multiple learning difficulties. Relevant practical strategies are suggested under each heading, but many of these techniques are suitable for a wide range of students. The final section presents projects that have been used successfully with pupils with learning difficulties.

Illustrating texts

Illustrations can bring a text to life and convey scenes and events to students who have difficulties understanding language. The illustrated versions of classics readily available may be suitable for students with reasonable vision who have the intellectual ability to grasp complex visual details. However, not many have pictures that are large and clear enough for students with learning difficulties to relate to the text.

To produce your own illustrations, you could:

- Ask art students from a local school or college to provide some large pictures to illustrate your text.
- Trace the outlines of pictures in books onto overhead transparencies and project them.
- Dress the students in costume and form tableaux of particular scenes. Photograph these, and project them as colour slides, or use a digital camera to capture the image on computer.

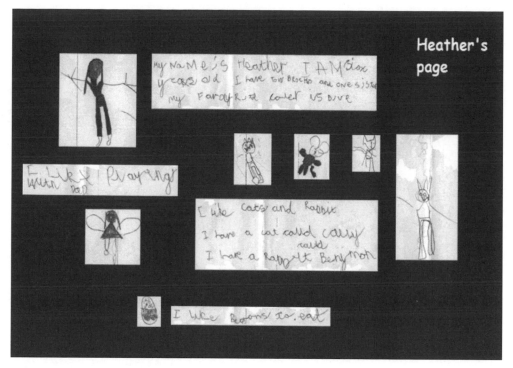

Figure 4.1 Heather's page

- Make simple outlines of characters, buildings, etc. from felt and use them on a felt board. You can move the characters around to represent different scenes in the story. Figure 4.1 shows a felt board created for 'Lord Randal', a border ballad.
- Create personal books for the students, with simple illustrations/tracings and the text in simple words or symbols (see p. xx).
- Create animations with drawings, simple puppets or animation software. If the students invest time and thought in creating the illustrations, the animation may be more meaningful to them than a commercial production.

Figure 4.2 'Lord Randal'.
Original drawing by Ghislane Grove
Photography by Mike Coles

LORD RANDAL (a Scottish traditional ballad)

Oh where have you been, Lord Randal my son?
Oh where have you been, my bonny young one?
Oh I've been to the greenwood, mother make my bed soon
For I'm weary with hunting and I fain would lie down.

And who did you meet there, Lord Randal my son?
And who did you meet there, my bonny young one?
Oh I met with my sweetheart, mother make my bed soon
For I'm weary with hunting and I fain would lie down.

What had you for your supper, Lord Randal my son?
What had you for your supper, my bonny young one?
Eels in eel broth, mother make my bed soon
For I'm weary with hunting and I fain would lie down.

What happened to your bloodhounds, Lord Randal my son?
What happened to your bloodhounds, my bonny young one?
They stretched out their legs and died, mother make my bed soon
For I'm weary with hunting and I fain would lie down.

Oh I fear you are poisoned, Lord Randal my son.
I fear you are poisoned, my bonny young one.
Oh yes, I am poisoned, mother make my bed soon
For I'm sick to my heart and I fain would lie down.

What will you leave your mother, Lord Randal my son?
What will you leave your mother, my bonny young one?
My house and my lands, mother make my bed soon
For I'm sick to my heart and I fain would lie down.

What will you leave your sweetheart, Lord Randal my son?
What will you leave your sweetheart, my bonny young one?
Yon tow and yon halter, mother, that hangs on yon tree.
And there let her hang, for the killing of me.

Film and audio tapes

There are good film versions of many novels and plays. Be selective and take time to decide which version will be most accessible to your students. For example, teacher Jane Grecic found that students enjoyed the old black and white film of *Hound of the Baskervilles* more than a recent version in colour, because the story was told more simply and obviously (see page 47). Cartoon versions may be more difficult than dramatisations, because emotions and interactions between characters are not so clearly visible, and a lot of inference may be required to bridge from one frame to another.

It is important not to make any assumptions about students' ability to understand material presented on film. The following strategies may be useful.

Using film as a teaching tool

- Watch the whole film (perhaps divided into parts to correspond to lessons) and then go back and revisit extracts as you work through the text in lessons.
- Use the 'layering' technique. Break the story down into small episodes or scenes, complete in themselves, and start each week by repeating an earlier episode or 'layer'. For example, you could tell the relevant part of the story to the group, then alert students to particular features to look for in the film, then show the scene, then review it to see what students have remembered.
- Once students are familiar with the film, use the 'pause' button to freeze the film and ask students what is happening, and what will happen next. (If you do this the first time the film is shown it is very distracting, and students never get a feel for the whole story.)

You can use audio tapes in a similar way. Many are commercially available, or you can make your own, recording different people reading the same poem, for example, or taking different parts in a narrative or drama. You can use the same strategies as for film, as well as the following:

Using audio tapes

- Play a poem to students to allow them to appreciate rhythms and pattern.
- Play extracts to students as a listening exercise. Use the pause technique (as for film).
- Add sound effects or actions to accompany the text on the tape.

Some books and poems are now available on CD-ROM, which allows you to select and replay visual and auditory images. (See Appendix 3: Teaching resources.)

Practical activities linked to texts

The following techniques may be helpful in encouraging students to engage with texts.

Story maps

These summarise the main events of the narrative and can be created as an OHP transparency or wall display, with arrows showing the links between events. A marker can be used to indicate the part of the story covered in the lesson. Students can predict alternative developments, which can be shown as a 'crossroad' with a question mark over it (see Figure 4.3).

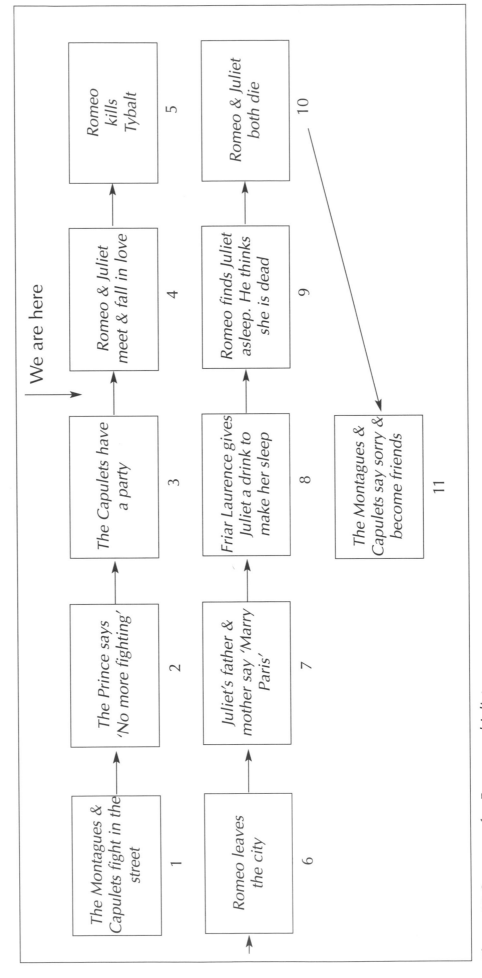

We are here

The Montagues & Capulets fight in the street	The Prince says 'No more fighting'	The Capulets have a party
1	2	3

Romeo & Juliet meet & fall in love	Romeo kills Tybalt	
4	5	

Romeo leaves the city	Juliet's father & mother say 'Marry Paris'	Friar Laurence gives Juliet a drink to make her sleep
6	7	8

Romeo finds Juliet asleep. He thinks she is dead	Romeo & Juliet both die	The Montagues & Capulets say sorry & become friends
9	10	11

Figure 4.3 Story map for *Romeo and Juliet*

Story boards

In film making, these are used to plan film sequences. Each main event is depicted on a separate sheet or board – in any way that students will recognise, for example simple line drawing and writing; props or objects, photographs.

This can encourage students to summarise the main events, and think about what they would include if they were filming the story. Once a story board has been created, you can film the scene, or get the students to form a tableau for a photograph.

Hot-seating

This technique can be used while enacting a scene from a text. Pause the action and invite characters to take a chair and be interviewed about their views of what is going on in the story.

News reports

While enacting a scene, pause the action. Students take turns to report on the events in the story, using a roving microphone to interview characters. They can present their reports and drawings in newspaper form.

Character maps

Create a map for an individual character using drawing, collage, silhouettes, photographs, etc. The map can represent the character's physical appearance and also their personality, using lists, symbols, props, etc.

You can also map the links between characters. Represent each main character in the text and link them using circles, ribbons, arrows, or move cut-outs physically, to illustrate the relationships between them. Group characters according to their roles in the story, for example 'good' versus 'bad' characters. (See Figure 4.4.)

Board games

Create a board game to show the events in the story, and what happens to the characters. Players can take on the role of characters, whose counters move up and down the board depending on their fortunes. This is particularly good for adventure stories and journeys, such as *The Hobbit*, or *Pilgrim's Progress*.

For a board game based on *Pilgrim's Progress*, achievements translate to advances along the board and disasters to delays or reversals:

- You have fallen into the Slough of Despond. Miss a turn
- You have left your scroll halfway down the Hill of Difficulty. Go back three spaces to retrieve it.
- You have arrived at the Palace Beautiful. Have another turn.

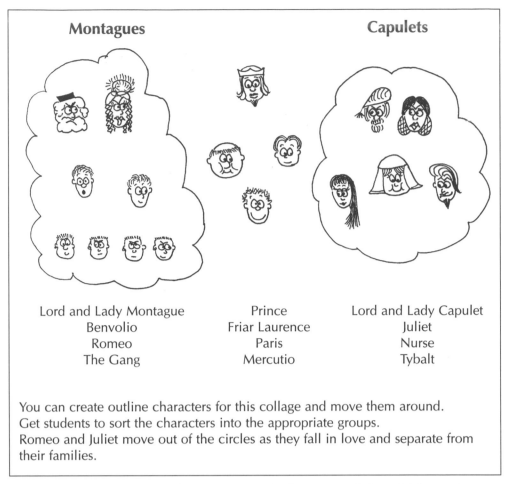

Montagues

Capulets

Lord and Lady Montague   Prince   Lord and Lady Capulet
Benvolio   Friar Laurence   Juliet
Romeo   Paris   Nurse
The Gang   Mercutio   Tybalt

You can create outline characters for this collage and move them around.
Get students to sort the characters into the appropriate groups.
Romeo and Juliet move out of the circles as they fall in love and separate from
their families.

Figure 4.4 Character map for *Romeo and Juliet,* artwork by Ghislaine Grove

The game can also be used to explore motivation and character, by predicting whether the people Pilgrim encounters are friends or foes. You could turn up character cards and guess, moving on a space if you are correct.

● Mr Worldly Wise says he knows how to help you – just follow him along this easy path. Will you go or not?

● You are in the ground of Giant Despair's castle. Do you think it will be a good idea to ask if you can stay the night?

Character inventions

Use what you know of a character to invent information, such as imaginary dialogues, attributes, possessions.

● What they would eat for dinner?
● What would she have in her handbag?
● What would he say if you met him?

Be careful not to be too anachronistic (for example, 'What football team does Tybalt support?'), as this could be confusing for some pupils.

Story packs

There are now many story packs commercially available, which include props that illustrate the story (see Appendix 3). Usually these are designed for primary-age children, but there is nothing to stop you creating your own set of resources for any text you want to use. Make sure that the props are stored properly in boxes and clearly labelled, and that you have enough sets of objects for each story. In the long run duplicates will be more economical than using one object in several stories (you will never be able to find it when you need it).

Teaching strategies across the range of special educational needs

'Special educational needs' is a blanket term which includes a very wide range of difficulties in language and learning. Norwich (1996) has suggested that we should think of three types of educational need:

- *needs of all children* – for example, to feel secure and to have their experiences recognised and validated
- *needs of individuals* – particular children will have their own likes and dislikes, styles of learning and experiences which are unique to them
- *needs which are common to groups* – in this case, different types of difficulty which have certain features in common.

In this section, we will identify some of the main categories of learning difficulties which have particular characteristics, and consider the implications for work with literature.

Moderate–severe learning difficulties

The term 'learning difficulties' is a general description of problems in adaptive functioning. In severe to profound learning difficulties, cognitive and linguistic impairments often result from damage to the developing brain. The precise nature of the learning difficulty depends on what has been affected and on the experiences and opportunities to learn that the child has had. There may be associated impairments to vision, hearing or motor skills, medical problems such as epilepsy, and psychological disturbances such as autism, as well as specific language difficulties.

As a broad generalisation, students with learning difficulties are likely to have short attention spans. They tend to have difficulty remembering information, generalising from one context to another and handling abstract concepts. Such students generally find it easier to understand language that is associated with everyday, meaningful events than language which is abstract and out of context. They may become confused when bombarded with too much information at a time, finding it easier to process information given in short chunks and repeated frequently and consistently.

Their expressive language tends to be at the level of simple sentences, perhaps using only one or two words at a time. Vocabulary is often dominated by concrete, familiar terms, mainly nouns. Students with severe speech impairments may use augmentative and alternative communication systems such as manual signs or gestures, books and aids with pictures or graphic symbols.

In conversation, students often find it hard to initiate and maintain turns, or to understand the different ways in which language is adapted and used in social situations. At a personal level, those who do not have additional emotional/behavioural problems often form close and loving relationships, and can understand and express a full range of feelings from humour and enjoyment to intense sadness.

Many students will be able to play symbolically and enjoy drama and role-play. For others, there should be no demand to pretend; instead they should be provided with a clearly defined real experience to which they have only to *respond*.

These common patterns of learning difficulties suggest certain strategies for using literature with such students (see panel below).

Successful strategies for students with moderate–severe learning difficulties

- Keep sessions short, or break up sessions into short episodes.
- Present information in a clear and structured way.

Use sensory cues to gain attention, aid memory and establish atmosphere (smell, taste, touch, sight and sound), but ensure the cues are not overwhelming.

- Reinforce listening by doing. For example, teach a catchphrase or an action for the whole group to repeat at certain points in the story. Find elements that can be acted, mimed or dramatised by small groups of students.
- Prepare carefully. Tell students something of what the story is about and who the characters are before you start. Have pictures and props ready to illustrate the story.
- Use repetition. Stories become familiar and accrue meaning through repeated experience. This allows students to build up a network of associations, and will make it easier for them to anticipate what is happening and to participate. Once the overall framework is familiar, you can vary elements within it to maintain interest and attention.
- Assemble the story gradually by 'layering'. Break it down into small episodes, complete in themselves, and start each week by repeating an earlier episode or 'layer' until the students are thoroughly familiar with it.
- Alternatively, start with a complete, but very simple outline of the story. Once the students are familiar with this, gradually build in elaboration.

- Make the transitions between one event and the next very clear.
- Emphasise the feeling and emotional aspects of the text.
- Simplify character and story line. Be ruthless in cutting out elements that are irrelevant to your main theme, or too complex.
- Create and display a story map (see page 32). Establish where on the map you are in each session.
- Identify character types. In many dramas and stories there are 'stock' characters such as the lovers, the villain, the clown, and you can often slot characters into these roles. Give each character an identifying feature, such as a prop, or a sign.
- Create character maps (see page 34) to show the links between characters, or their roles in the story.
- Give students opportunities to generalise their understanding of the story through associated activities in other areas of the curriculum, such as art and music.
- Program lines from stories or poems on to simple switch-operated communication aids, or language masters. Any story or poem with a repetitive refrain offers a good starting point. Repeated refrains can also be used when characters appear, or at the beginning or end of the session.

> *Examples of repetitive refrains*
>
> I'll huff and I'll puff and I'll blow your house down.
> *(Three Little Pigs)*
>
> And still she sat, and still she reeled, and still she wished for company
> ('The Strange Guest', Scottish traditional poem)
>
> Far and few, far and few
> Are the lands where the Jumblies live
> Their heads are green and their hands are blue
> And they went to sea in a sieve.
> (Edward Lear, 'The Jumblies')
>
> 'What saw thou there?' said the King.
> 'Sir, I saw nothing but the waters wap and the waves wan.'
> (Thomas Malory, 'Morte d'Arthur')

Autistic spectrum

Autism is a spectrum of particular features that can affect individuals across the ability range. Autistic students generally find it hard to see the world from the point of view of others and to interpret emotions and social behaviour. Their interactions tend to be instrumental (getting things done for me) rather than motivated by the desire to share information and feelings with others. Other common features are over-literal understanding, difficulties with symbolic play and ritualistic obsessions. Students with autism can relate to the world of things, and do not necessarily have problems understanding means–end relations such as tool use, or the substitution of one set of features for another. Thus some individuals can engage in a limited form of symbolic play (making a matchbox into a car, for example), but they may find it much harder to take on roles, or understand the symbolic meanings related to others' experience.

Individuals at the severe end of the spectrum may fail to develop language, or use only a few words or signs, often imitated rather than spontaneous. Others may have sophisticated pronunciation and grammar but have little understanding of the social use of language. Because their understanding tends to be very literal, people with autism find it hard to discern double meanings such as sarcasm, jokes or metaphors. Their difficulties with determining what information is relevant for another person can lead to over-specific answers (describing what they did yester-day in minute detail) or under-specific (answering 'Yes' to a caller who asks 'Is your mum home?').

Students with autism tend to have a limited understanding and use of terms to do with feelings and mental states (thinking, believing, know-ing, imagining, etc.). They may be able to describe what happened in a narrative, but not what it meant to the participants. However, they may have good rote memories for lines of poetry, enjoy the sound of words in rhymes and nonsense verse, and like word play and word associations. Where personal relationships are concerned, the classic descriptions of autism suggest an incapacity to feel or form bonds. However, more recent insights suggest that autistic individuals may be attached to their families, and long to form friendships, but lack the knowledge and skills of how to do so appropriately, or how to show their feelings (see, for example, Peter and Sherratt-Smith 2001).

The characteristics associated with autism suggest that there will be certain aspects of literature that these students will find difficult, partic-ularly in the interplay of character and narrative. While they may be able to follow a story, it will be very hard for them to interpret motivation and predict consequences, or to empathise imaginatively with what is going on. Approaches to literature that start by creating an emotional atmos-phere may be less effective than approaches that emphasise explicit logical patterns, and the sound and rhythms of words. It is important to be sensitive to obsessions – some students may have idiosyncratic phobias or fads which you may need to take account of in planning. For example, if you are doing *Macbeth* and one of the students has a real obsession with knives, you might choose to avoid the daggers, or use very crude cardboard shapes.

Despite the difficulties, literature offers a rich source of opportunities for working directly on some of the social skills that these students need. Most of the strategies suggested for pupils with learning disabilities (see page 35) will be relevant for students with autistic spectrum disorders.

Other books which focus on teaching social cognition to children with autism include: *Teaching Children with Autism to Mind-read* by Pat Howlin, and *Social Cognition Through Literature and drama with Children who have Autistic Spectrum Disorders: Macbeth in Mind* by Nicola Grove and Keith Park.

Successful strategies for students with autism

- Be careful not to overload students with too many sensory inputs – take into consideration the way they process informa-tion, and their likes and dislikes, when you are planning how to illustrate the story.

- Make things explicit. Bring out the motivation of characters, and explain the difference between what people think, what people feel and how they behave. Use picture symbols with illustrations of the characters to show how they are feeling: sad, worried, happy, etc. Different shaped 'bubbles' can represent thought, feeling and speech (see the story board on page 40).

- Exaggerate displays of emotion, so that students can see the contrasts clearly.

- Provide prompts to enable students to rehearse pretend events. For example, students can sequence photographs of key events in a drama, which they then re-enact.

- Use cues to structure discussion about the text. For example, use fake 'remote control' as a cue to stop the action or the story-telling and then ask questions such as 'What's going to happen next?, 'Why did s/he do that?'

- Translate the story or drama into a board game that has clear formal rules, to help pupils access the events (see page 33).

- Use images to help students understand key features of narratives, characters or scenes. For example, images traditionally associated with the countryside or city, which may be cliches, can help students to fix on something essential. (See Figure 4.5.)

- Music can be very useful to establish atmosphere and to carry the text – for example, saying 'A drum, a drum, Macbeth doth come' very rhythmically to a drum beat. Use sound, such as scary music, chase music, or the rippling scales that indicate a flashback in time.

- Devise games and tasks to explore metaphor and figurative language. For example, identify visual similarities between objects – as white as snow, as soft as silk. In *Macbeth*, we used a flower and a toy snake to illustrate how a snake might lie concealed beneath a flower, just as Macbeth's smiling face concealed his murderous intention.

- Present the sessions in a consistent structure, so that students become familiar with a way to approach and understand stories. For example, develop routines to begin and end a session.

- You may need to avoid heightening emotions and atmosphere as this may overload the student. You can gradually build up to more dramatic presentations, starting very low key if needed.

> Other very helpful approaches to develop imaginative response can be found in Melanie Peter and Dave Sherratt-Smith's book *Developing Spontaneous Play in Children with Autism*.

Specific language impairments

This term describes students who have particular problems with understanding or expressive language, over and above what would be expected from their levels of achievement in other areas. One or more aspects of language may be affected.

- *Vocabulary and word meanings:* difficulties with finding the right word, or understanding the range of meanings of a word.

- *Grammar:* difficulties with constructing well-formed utterances: grammatical elements may be left out, or put in the wrong places.

- *Pronunciation:* difficulties with producing, and possibly perceiving, speech sounds, so that speech is hard to understand.

Figure 4.5 Thinking, feeling and saying bubbles

- *social use of language:* may use language inappropriately, and find difficulty in managing both verbal and non-verbal aspects of conversation.

Expressive language is often more severely affected than comprehension. Problems with understanding may not be apparent in everyday conversation where there are many contextual cues. However, students may find stories difficult to interpret because of the several demands on attention and on the ability to make inferences and integrate information into a cohesive whole. They may find interpreting idiom difficult simply because they do not know whether the use in a given context is idiomatic or literal. For example, a student who can match a picture showing 'happiness' with the expression 'full of beans' may interpret 'full of beans' literally in context, because he does not expect idiomatic language to be used in a particular social situation (the same problems are often experienced by people with autistic spectrum disorders).

The strategies described below are grouped according to particular difficulties students may have.

Successful strategies for students with specific language impairments

Techniques traditionally used to help poor readers understand written texts can also be applied to oral comprehension.

- Focus on cue words in the text that allow you to infer missing information. For example, 'Helen lay in bed, listening to the sounds of her mother preparing breakfast in the kitchen downstairs.' This tells us that Helen is a girl, she lives with her mother, it is early morning, she will probably get up and eat her breakfast soon.

- Ask Who? Why? What? questions to generate information. Start with sentences, building up to paragraphs and whole stories.

- Encourage students to summarise the main points of a story they have heard.

- Omit key sections from a story and ask students to identify what is missing.

- Use mental imagery. Start by providing an illustration (see page 28) that students can recall when they describe the story. With experience, students can create their own mental pictures.

The following techniques may be helpful for students who have difficulties learning, recalling and interpreting vocabulary.

- Explain words with difficult meanings by giving a simpler equivalent that is within the student's vocabulary.

- Emphasise the emotional and rhythmic aspects of unfamiliar text, to build up a sense of the meaning

- Focus on the words that the student really needs to know in order to grasp the meaning (for example, names of characters and places).
- Use riddles and descriptive poetry. These can provide useful opportunities for building up associations and getting students to attend to and retrieve word meanings.
- Use word substitution games, similes and metaphors. These help students to build up networks of meaning and thus explore the meaning of a text.
- Focus on quotations from the text to build up a foundation of understanding, leading to comprehension of the whole text.

Students who have difficulty with pronunciation may find it difficult to recognise complex or unfamiliar words, and will find any oral recitation a challenge.

- Encourage students to:
  - put speeches into their own words
  - mime or gesture difficult passages
  - use tape recordings or communication aids with their own or others' voices
  - join in group recitals with one well-chosen word or phrase.
- Focus on the rhythm and intonation of a piece, without worrying too much about the exact pronunciation of individual words, to help improve intelligibility.

Students who have problems with the social use of language can be helped by the strategies suggested for students with autism (see page 38).

Hearing impairments

Many individuals with severe hearing impairments do not get sufficient input in a comprehensible form during the critical period of language acquisition, leading to difficulties in understanding complex language. Information needs to be presented visually and through movement.

Successful strategies for students with hearing impairments

- Use clear pictorial illustrations, felt boards, etc. (see page 29).
- Create a visual story map (see page 32).
- Create character maps for individuals to represent relationships between them (see page 34).
- Illustrate scenes with pictures or collage, using colour symbolically

(for example, red for love, passion, anger; black for grief; yellow for happiness, etc.).

- Use mime, gesture, signs and symbols to convey meaning, but take care in translation. A pedantic emphasis on word-for-word rendition is more likely to obscure the sense of a passage than to clarify it (see Appendix 2).

- Use dance and movement as creative routes to meaning. Explore ways of moving to the rhythm of a poem, or conveying its meaning through actions and movement.

- People with hearing impairments are increasingly creating their own poetry in sign and signed versions of poems, which rely on the form of the sign to create visual and dynamic effects.

Dual sensory impairments and profound learning difficulties

People with profound learning difficulties may have both visual and auditory impairments and rely on touch, taste and smell to gain information about the world. They need to be given plenty of space and time to understand what is happening. Because students may have unpredictable responses to sensory stimuli, such as tactile-defensiveness, it is important to base your planning for their involvement on individual needs and preferences.

Individuals with profound learning difficulties are usually functioning at a pre-language and pre-symbolic level of development, and may not be communicating intentionally. They are heavily reliant on others to interpret their needs and interests. The onus is therefore on you as story-teller to create meanings for the student at whatever level is appropriate.

Successful strategies for students with dual sensory impairments and/or profound learning difficulties

- Use smell cues. These have to be planned carefully because some smells linger on, and too many smells are confusing. Use one smell, such as mint, to signify the beginning and the ending of a session, and another to convey a particular atmosphere – for example, coconut oil for a desert island, burnt porridge for the opening scene of *Oliver Twist*. Be careful about food smells if you are not planning to give people the same food to eat, as this may raise hopes or confuse with everyday events such as coffee time or dinner.

- Use tactile cues. Make sure that there are some concrete representations to illustrate a story, character or poem, such as contrasting fabrics, or objects to handle. *Bag Books* are specially created stories told through the medium of physical objects on a large page, and are very successful with both children and adults. For example in 'Granny's visit', the children feel and manipulate a

---

'Tarantella' by Hilaire Belloc is a really rhythmic poem. If you say bits of it really close up to someone's back or neck, they can feel the difference between the short, quick tappy sounds illustrating the dancer:

And the Hip! Hop! Hap!
And the clap
Of the hands to the twirl and
* the swirl*
Of the girl gone chancing
Glancing
Dancing
Backing and advancing
Snapping of the clapper to
* the spin*
Out and in

and the long, sad vowels of the last stanza, which have lots of humming and low sounds:

Nevermore Miranda,
* nevermore...*
No sound
Only the boom
Of the far Waterfall like
* Doom.*

Odyssey Now, by Nicola Grove and Keith Park, was designed to include students who have dual sensory impairments and/or profound learning difficulties, and provides a planning framework for organising sensory information, and for organising groups based on the needs and levels of functioning of individual students.

letter box (actual size) as the text about a letter coming through the door is read; later they get to use a duster and real polish to help Mum get the house clean (see Appendix 3).

- Encourage physical participation. Think about dramatising stories and poems through different kinds of touch and movement. For example, Romeo and Juliet's first meeting involves a palm-to-palm touch; in the Zeffirelli film they strain to touch hands from the balcony. Their linked hands can be dragged apart by their respective families to dramatise their separation.

- Lie students on a 'resonance board' (see Appendix 3 for instructions on how to make this) and tap it in rhythm with the language of the text. This helps them feel the language through their whole body. Alternatively, you can hold small children on your lap, or position people against your own body, and say the words rhythmically onto their back, emphasising the contrasting sounds.

- Keep the pace slow. Plan at first to do only one or two activities in a session, and build up gradually.

Into the classroom

Teachers, therapists and learning support assistants all over the country are experimenting with literature. Most are too busy to put their ideas in writing, which is a shame because we can all benefit from each other's creativity and ideas. The following accounts illustrate approaches that have proved successful with a range of students. Once you get really interested, almost any text you can think of has something to offer.

Gulliver's Travels

The following ideas, based on *Gulliver's Travels*, have been used successfully with a group who needed work on social skills.

Journey to Lilliput

Emphasise the size difference between Gulliver and the little people of the island.

- Show a dolls' house bed and ask, 'How many of these put together would Gulliver need?'
- Show a dolls' house cup, fill it with water, and ask, 'Would this be enough water for you?'
- Show a handkerchief and tell students that it is a Lilliputian's sheet: 'How many would it take to make a sheet big enough for Gulliver?'
- Ask the group to 'shrink'. Throw a large blanket or sheet over the group and explain that this is what Gulliver's handkerchief was like to the little people.

Illustrate the factionalism between the Blefuscans and the Lilliputians.

- Find out from the group something that divides them. For example, in one group, one person liked Robbie Williams while another hated him but liked Daniel Bedingfield. The group then naturally split itself into two factions supporting the different singers, with one leader per group.
- Encourage the two factions to argue about the issue and make sweeping generalisations. For example, all those who like Robbie Williams are boring, silly people who should be locked up.
- Choose a student in one group to be the king. This group is the more powerful one, and the king can put the others in prison (a ring of chairs) and force them to wear badges to single them out. Is it fair that these people should be treated like that, because they like different music?
- Encourage the factions to resolve the dispute, without resorting to violence.

Note: In *New Horizons* (see Appendix 3), speech and language therapist Carolyn Fyfe has developed a series of 'themed groups' on the topic of adventures in literature. These include ideas for working with *The Hobbit*, *The Odyssey* and *Gulliver's Travels*.

A Christmas Carol

Rosie Brown developed a series of lessons for a group of students with moderate, severe and profound learning difficulties.

Scrooge and Bob Cratchit

Scene: Bob Cratchit asks Scrooge for the day off on Christmas Day, and wishes him a Merry Christmas.

Theme: Unwillingness to share; contrast between meanness and generosity.

Activities

- In pairs, pupils take the roles of Bob Cratchit and Scrooge. Bob asks for money, Scrooge refuses and sends him away. Bob says 'Merry Christmas', and Scrooge says 'Bah! Humbug!' (use a simple communication aid for pupils with no speech). After a time, pupils reverse roles.

- For pupils with profound learning difficulties: adults offer something, then snatch it away, saying 'Bah! Humbug!'

Skills: Working in pairs, role-playing different feelings and behaviour, asking for things.

Resources: Black cloak for Scrooge, tinsel for Bob, money bags. Dim the lights and use gloomy music to create atmosphere.

Art work: Christmas decorations and display of words offered by pupils to describe Scrooge.

The Hound of the Baskervilles

Jane Grecic developed a series of lessons over several weeks on *The Hound of the Baskervilles* with a group of Key Stage 3 pupils.

- Sessions followed a similar format each week.
  - Students started in the classroom, recapping on the story so far, sometimes by doing short pieces of drama in small groups or completing worksheets. Pupils with profound and multiple learning difficulties were provided with sensory activities such as massage to music using props from 'the moor', or following sensory trails as clues.
  - The group crossed the 'grimpen mire' (green paper towels representing the safe grassy path across the moor), assisting their peers across and shouting encouragement. They entered a darkened room, lit only by candlelight.
  - The teacher told the story, using sensory props to build up the atmosphere week by week, for example listening to wind sounds, putting on hats and scarves to keep warm, and feeling the soil and leaves. The language used for the story was a mixture of a simplified version, passages of original text from an audiotape version, and pupils' own retelling.

- Students played interactive games, including:
  - *Grandmother's Footsteps* – the student at the front was the hound with a piece of fur fabric; others had to sneak up without being heard.

   – *Hide and seek* – the 'hound' hid in the dark, wearing the fur, while others took turns to try and find him or her by listening to where the howling was coming from (the sound was programmed on to a Big Mack switch where necessary).

● Students looked for clues. The concepts of detectives and clues were explained, and then the pupils were offered a reward (a sweet) for having worked so hard. However, when she came to look, the teacher discovered that the sweets were missing from her bag. Pupils followed a trail of clues (written, pictorial and sensory) to hunt for the missing sweets.

Worksheets

These were a mixture of pictures to colour, opportunities for free drawing, and copy writing. They were made into individual books for pupils.

Resources

Candle lantern; sound effects tapes for wind noises, wolf howls; electric fan for wind; bowl of potting compost, leaves, twigs; green paper towels for the path across the moor; black fur fabric for the Hound; long bristly brush (its paw); 'Dragon's breath' bottled smell for its breath (any disgusting smell will do); hats and scarves for costumes.

Teacher's comments

I am still amazed at the amount of information about the story that pupils have remembered. The 'big bad dog' has become a bit of a joke in school, as I was, and still am, literally 'hounded' by pupils asking for it again. I feel the success of the book lay in the fact that it was a thriller – each week, pupils were taken to the point of total terror and back again in complete safety (similar to riding the big dipper). The anticipation of the session for many pupils started with them asking/signing to me about it as they got off the transport on a Monday morning, and this continued throughout the week until the session on a Friday morning (it even helped some of our pupils learn the days of the week!).

'Kubla Khan'

Sally Blackah, Joanna Sebire and Sue Brady worked on Coleridge's 'Kubla Khan' for a term with a class of 14–15-year-old students with specific language impairments. They chose the poem for its visual nature and fantastical imagery. The work involved using a mixture of sensory inputs – visual, auditory and tactile – and was a meaningful introduction to pre-twentieth-century literature.

The pleasure dome

- The poem was read aloud several times in its entirety, to put the quotations (see below) in context within the narrative. The style of delivery was dramatic, to help the students access the atmosphere of the poem.
- The students were divided into two groups to work on displays, one on 'paradise' and one on 'hell'. To evoke an emotional response, 'dark' music was played to the 'hell' group and 'light' music to the 'paradise' group. Students used images from the text and their own conceptual realisations to create a three-dimensional display.

Opposites

Quotations from the text, printed and enlarged, were classified as positive or negative.

For example:

Positive	*Negative*
'fertile land'	'close your eyes with holy dread'
'deep delight'	'turmoil'
'blossomed many an incense bearing tree'	'ancestral voices prophesying war'

This activity led to much discussion about opposites and extremes. Certain quotations were much more difficult to classify because of the conflicting imagery, for example 'a sunny pleasure dome with caves of ice'. This led to further discussion about differences of opinion, and the recognition that certain things cannot be easily categorised.

Drawing

Students drew the dome and its surrounding areas to represent positive aspects (inner calm) and negative aspects (turmoil), interpreting the written images visually.

Poetry workshop

A poetry workshop for younger pupils used Kit Wright's 'Red Boots On', H. H. Munro's 'Overheard on a Salt Marsh', and the traditional Scottish poem 'The Strange Guest'.

'Red Boots On'

The poem was adapted to include place names around Wigan where the children lived, and to include each child in the group in turn, using the colour of their footwear. The rest of the group clapped the rhythm of the poem:

Original text	*Adapted text*
Way down Geneva	Way down Kingsbury
All along Vine	Along Tontine
Deeper than the snowdrift	Deeper than the snowdrift
Love's eyes shine	Love's eyes shine
Mary Lou's walking	Kevin is walking
In the wintertime	In the wintertime
She's got	He's got
Red boots on	Black shoes on
She's got	He's got
Red boots on	Black shoes on
Kicking up the winter,	Kicking up the winter,
till the winter's gone.	till the winter's gone.

'Overheard on a Saltmarsh'

Nymph, Nymph, what are your beads?
Green glass, goblin. Why do you stare at them?
Give them me.
    No.
Give them me. Give them me.
        No . . .

Some real 'green glass beads' on a necklace were held out for pupils to reach towards and touch. The group joined in with the refrains 'Give them me' and 'No', using speech, sign and communication aids. The one pupil who did not seem to be enjoying the experience temporarily took on the role of the goblin lying howling in the reeds.

'The Strange Guest'

A wife was sitting at her reel one night.
And still she sat, and still she reeled, and still she wished for
company.
In came a pair of big, big feet, and sat down at the fireside;
And still she sat, and still she reeled, and still she wished for
company.
In came a pair of small, small knees, and sat down on the big,
big feet.
And still she sat, and still she reeled, and still she wished for
company...

A member of staff drew the parts of the appearing troll as they were
named in the poem while pupils pointed to their own body parts.

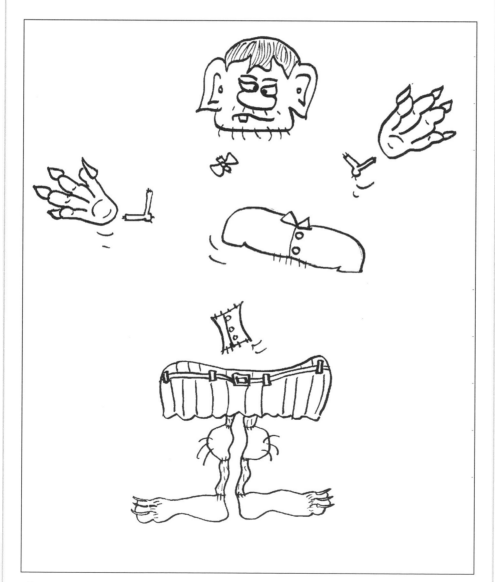

Figure 4.6 Original drawing by Chislaine Grove

'Wind' by Ted Hughes

Jane Grecic's students studied poems about the wind, focusing on the Ted Hughes poem.

Students listened to the poem read by their teacher and by other male and female readers on home-made tapes. The class worked through the poem in a different way each week, first exploring sound effects, then visual images (a huge art session), and finally as drama.

For sound effects, students had a range of musical instruments as well as common objects to create sounds with, for example by wobbling large sheets of card.

For visual images they painted large banners to represent the sea and the orange sky.

For drama they mimed activities such as walking in the wind.

Other physical activities included kite flying, wind walks, using electric fans and making paper fans, windmills and model magpies hung from elastic fixed to sticks which were then flung as described in the poem.

At noon I scaled along the house side as far as
The coal-house door. Once I looked up –
Through the brunt wind that dented the balls of my eyes.

We watch the fire blazing
And feel the roots of the house move, but sit on
Seeing the window tremble to come in
Hearing the stones cry out under the horizons.

We ended by making toast

Figure 4.7

The group discussed the setting for the poem, and then visited Jane's house, which is a cottage on top of a hill with an open fire and a coal shed. This visit proved the highlight of the project. The students fetched coal from the shed, lit the fire, made toast and listened to the poem in the dark by firelight. They then went out into the garden and watched the wind blowing the smoke out of the chimney. The sensory aspects of the visit were recalled in school using firelighters, coal and kindling to help with recall.

The students completed simple worksheets with drawings and writings of themselves flying kites in the wind. However, one student insisted on drawing the poet himself, faithfully reproducing Jane's description of him as 'wild and hairy'.

Figure 4.8

Finally the students presented the poem in assembly, with some of them reading or accompanying particular lines

'WIND' – Ted Hughes
Bryn

This house has been far out at sea all night
Jessica and Kevin – sea picture

The woods crashing through the darkness, the booming hills
Sam – cymbal, Laura – drum

Winds stampeding the fields under the window

Floundering black astride and blinding wet
Bryn – water spray spraying audience

Till day rose: then under an orange sky
Jessica/Kevin – sky picture

The hills had new places, and wind wielded

Blade-light, luminous black and emerald,
Ian – moves around waving ribbon

Flexing like the lens of a mad eye.

At noon I scaled along the house-side as far as
Sam with coal skuttle

The coal house door. Once I looked up
Sam miming

Through the brunt wind that dented the balls of my eyes
Still Sam

The tent of hills drummed and strained its guyrope.
Laura/Bryn drumming

The fields quivering, the skyline a grimace,

At any second to bang and vanish with a flap
– tambourine

The wind flung a magpie away and a black
Victoria/Daniel – magpies

Back gull bent like an iron bar slowly. The house

Rang like some fine green goblet in the note
Victoria – triangle

That at any second would shatter it. Now deep

In chairs in front of the great fire, we grip

Our hearts and cannot entertain book, thought

Or each other. We watch the fire blazing,
Turn torches on

And feel the roots of the house move, but sit on

Seeing the window tremble to come in,
Daniel with card to shake

Hearing the stones cry out under the horizons
– rainmaker

Figure 4.9

CHAPTER 5
Getting started with creative writing

Tina Detheridge, Olivia O'Sullivan and Nicola Grove

> The stories of our days and the stories in our days are joined in that autobiography we are all engaged in making and remaking, as long as we live, which we never complete, though we all know how it is going to end.
>
> (Barbara Hardy, *Tellers and Listeners*)

The previous chapters have looked at ways in which students can 'read' literature, by taking part in a variety of activities that integrate their experiences and imagination with the text. With the right support, even students with severe disabilities may be able to respond creatively to what they have read, for example through art, dance, music or drama. As a creative response, writing has particular value, since the process of writing shapes the dynamics of language into permanent material form. In Chapter 4 we saw some examples of simple writing and drawing in response to literature. This chapter focuses on types and methods of producing writing, using text or symbols, and how these skills may be extended.

The power of writing

Writing is a means of expression, but the process of writing has many other functions.

- Writing is a mechanism for storing ideas. When I go shopping I write a list. The process of constructing the list helps to fix it in my mind, so that if I forget the list, I am still able to retrieve much of the information.

- Writing allows us to 'see' ideas, to sort and structure thoughts. If I listen to a lecture, particularly one that is quite difficult to understand, I write a lot of notes. I never read these notes. It is the act of translating someone else's ideas into note form, selecting and structuring the key points, which helps me to understand and internalise the new concepts.

- Writing stories or poetry is about structuring and manipulating experiences and emotions. It provides a way of reflecting on experience that can develop a sense of self, advance language skills, and facilitate participation in a culturally valued activity.

Young children create fantasies and stories in their play, talking with their dolls or playthings, imbuing them with reality. As they begin to distinguish between 'truth' and 'fantasy', many children gradually become inhibited in such self-expression. They may also lack the confidence or ability to handle the linguistics, to form letters, and to spell and understand syntax. By the time they reach adolescence, many children may find writing creatively a difficult and painful experience. However, if they can be encouraged to produce their thoughts and feelings in written form, they have a means of reflecting on experience which can develop a sense of self, advance language skills, and facilitate participation in a culturally valued activity, as the examples in this chapter show.

Being a writer, a creator of literature, confers a status on an individual. To be able to express your own ideas in writing is a dignifying process. Students can take their stories home and share their pleasure in their achievement with their parents and carers. Students who have had little opportunity to write, who may currently be unable physically to write, to recognise or spell words, or to handle syntax, or who find the whole bundle of processes too complex, will all be excluded from the world of writers. This chapter considers alternative forms of 'writing' and ways of enabling students to become 'authors' and experience the satisfaction that this confers.

A first experience of writing

Mabel is a chatty person, with plenty of ideas, but her sole communication is oral. She has a tendency to repeat herself to give weight to an idea. However, she is not able to read or write text. At the Mencap and Gateway Conference in 1997 she used an overlay keyboard attached to a computer to select symbols. She could relate to these illustrations, and with very little encouragement was able to choose and sequence them to create her own piece of writing. She listened to the text being spoken back by the computer, confirming her writing. When she was satisfied, her work was printed. It was a pity there was not a video camera on hand to capture her tremendous pleasure in holding this piece of writing, which gave permanent evidence of her ideas. She read the writing back by using the symbols as reminders of what she had said, which gave her the idea that she could read other things. She immediately marched across the hall to an author displaying his work, complaining that he had not put the symbols into his book for her to read!

Alternative forms of writing

The main alternatives to independent writing are to use symbols, computer technology and dictation, or a combination of the three.

Using symbols

Pictures and graphic symbols provide ways of expressing ideas in written, retrievable form for pupils who cannot read or write. Appendix 2 describes some of the systems of pictorial and conceptual symbols in common use.

A group of students at Wilson Stuart School, who are all communication aid users, wrote stories about their hopes and feelings, using symbols. Some of these stories were very moving, sometimes giving staff the first glimpse of the depth of feelings these children have. Keeping a sense of humour, having jokes and their responses programmed into the communication aids helped the children join in exchanges with their peers. Life can sometimes seem rather too serious if you are not given the tools to laugh, joke and mess around with.

Below are two illustrations of some of the very first stories they wrote in symbol form to convey something about who they were.

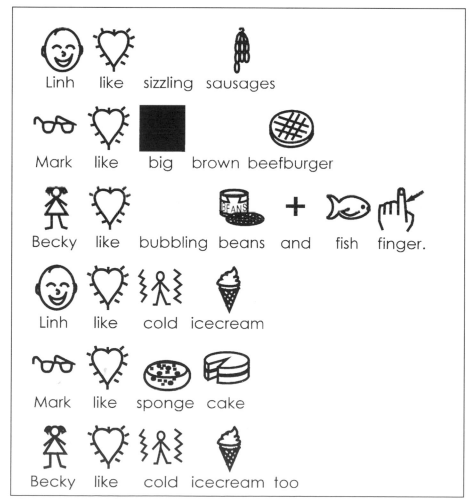

Figure 5.1(a) Wilson Stuart School communication group: exploring sounds and feelings

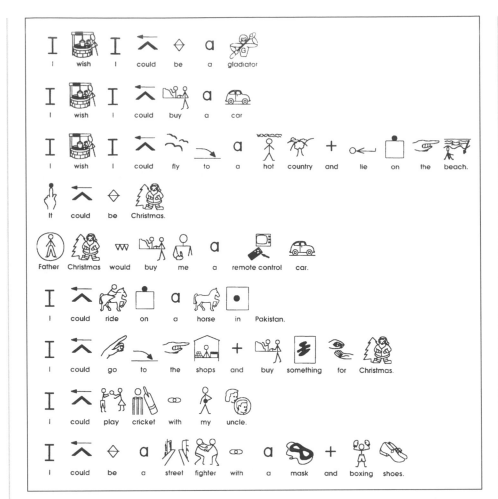

Figure 5.1(b) Wilson Stuart School: children's hopes and wishes

Each child's stories were put into non-reflective plastic wallets to make them more durable and stored in ring binders, so it was easy to turn the pages and other pages to be added. The children built up personal books about their lives and interests.

On the Symbolworld website (www.symbolworld.org) young writers can publish their own symbol-supported writing. This may be a personal story, a piece of collaborative work, or some non-fiction. Pupils at Ganton School worked together to symbolise the poem 'Tyger, Tyger'. They sent their work in, along with their own paintings, which were published on this website. As well as the satisfaction of seeing their work on-line, they are immensely proud of the fact that their work is used by hundreds of other pupils around the world. (See Figure 5.2.)

There are currently no (formal) syntactical or grammatical rules for symbols, so students can use and interpret them freely and creatively. For example, a student trying to explain in symbols that it was 'very windy' did so by repeating the symbol for windy, that is 'windy windy'. This is very expressive, but not grammatical in a formal sense.

Symbols can provide a bridge to literacy. Visual languages, such as signing and symbols, can help students make the leap from picture to

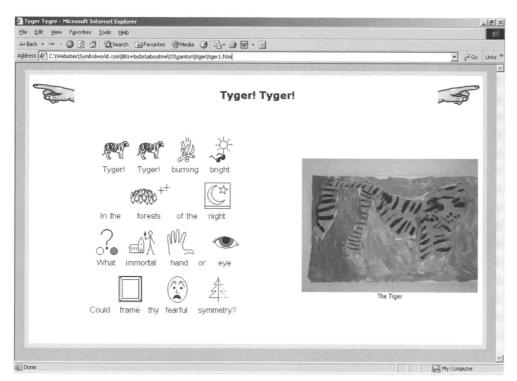

Figure 5.2 'Tyger Tyger' from Ganton on Symbolworld

Using symbols provides a way of:

- building self-esteem through almost instant success to reading
- developing an interest in reading and stories
- developing the use of context and syntax cues in reading
- developing phonological awareness
- picking out the main idea from a piece of text.

word and facilitate participation in a range of literacy activities. As they become familiar with the words, some of the symbols can be removed, leaving enough cues to enable the student to complete the activity, but at the same time giving them the chance to handle vocabulary.

Using symbols in playscripts

Shirley Austin, of Marshlands School, has written plays for her primary school pupils with special educational needs. One group wished to perform a fairly lengthy play about the Romans. The pupils would have found it hard to learn their parts without a great deal of help. Printing the text with symbol support meant that they could read the script.

At another school, the script for the Christmas play was printed with each part in a different colour, so that each character could identify their lines easily. Symbols were also used as prompts for the context.

These techniques helped students to identify when it was their turn to speak and gave them symbol cues to the content of their next speech. This ensured that the flow of the story kept along the right lines.

Making books

Students and teachers can make small story books, using a single sheet of A4 paper folded into four to make pages. Students dictate their story, or communicate it using signs or symbols, and the teacher writes it with one or two sentences on each page, supported with symbols as appropriate. These may be based on pupils' personal experiences, or a book or poem. Leave space on each page for the student to illustrate the writing, copy it or add more.

The students can then share their stories with others in the class and the text can be used in a variety of ways as a learning resource (see 'Structured writing activities based on familiar texts', p. 64).

Using technology

One of the joys of technology is that it can present components for writers to work from, rather than having to engage in the whole of the scribing process independently. It allows the author to focus on the literacy rather than the mechanics of writing. You will need some basic training in understanding different aspects of access technology and in using the various programs available in order to support young writers using technology. In all of the examples given, the teacher needs to prepare the grids used on overlays or computer screens, thus predetermining the vocabulary the pupil can access through the grids.

A range of useful computer programs is listed in Appendix 2.

Word banks and on-screen grids

Word banks with lists of words, perhaps supported by pictures, can act as a stimulus to writing or offer support for the writing process. An on-screen grid is a bank of words, pictures or phrases that are added to the document when the user clicks on them. They are particularly helpful for less confident writers who may be able to read but find it easier to select from a list rather than conjure up the word and its spelling. Similarly, on-screen grids with symbols and pictures can help writers who cannot read, or who have significant difficulty in writing using text.

On-screen grids

Programs that use on-screen grids will have instructions on how you can make the grids and add your own choice of vocabulary. The flexibility will depend on the software program used. For example, in Writing with Symbols or Clicker 4 you can put photographs, symbols pr pictures with words into a grid. Clicking on a cell can 'send' the message to the writing document. This process enables the writer to compose text from pre-defined words or phrases, possibly using symbols or pictures. The details of the functions will, of course, vary from one software program to another. A number of grids can be linked to give a dynamic access to a wide vocabulary.

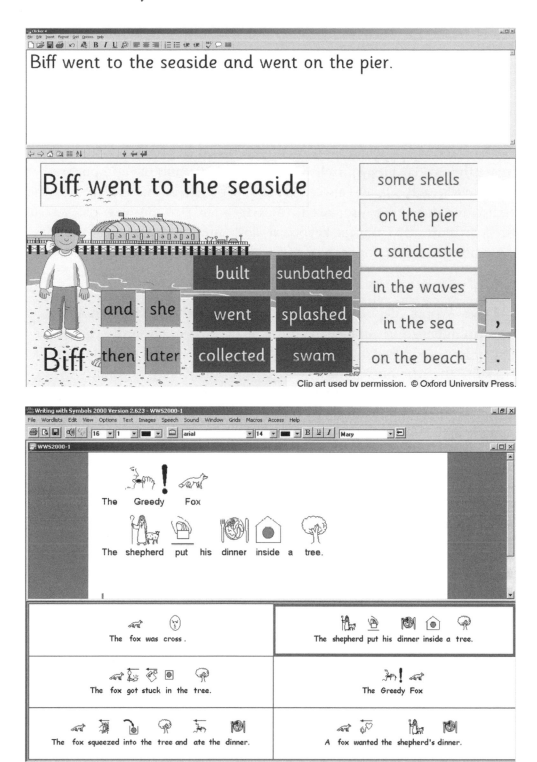

Figure 5.3 and 5.4 Retelling a story using on-screen grids, using Clicker 4 (top) and Writing with Symbols

On-screen grids can be operated by clicking on a cell in the grid or, if you have a touch-screen monitor, by touching the cell. They can also be used on whiteboards for direct access in a class situation. Alternatively on-screen keyboards can be set up to be operated by switches, for pupils who cannot use a keyboard.

Overlay keyboards

An alternative to an on-screen grid is an overlay keyboard. This is a separate device with a grid that plugs into the computer. The user can select different areas on the overlay to 'send' specific text to the program instead of typing from the keyboard. Overlay keyboards are usually supplied with a program that allows you to create the files that tell the computer what message to 'write' when an area of the board is pressed. You need to create the overlay files yourself (this is the file that tells the computer what to write for each cell, and also creates the paper sheet that is placed on the board to show the user what messages are). Examples of overlay keyboards are the Concept keyboard, and Intellitools. You can purchase the editing software for each of these with the boards.

> Dave Wood, deputy head teacher at Wilson Stuart School in Birmingham for pupils with physical disabilities, believes that the children need to experience storytelling before they can refine the skills. In their nursery the children use an overlay keyboard with symbol writing software to produce 'scribble' or 'pretend' writing before they even learn to recognise symbols as part of their emergent literacy experience. He also encourages the teachers to model the writing process, by writing in class, using the same technologies.

Text-to-speech programs

Using a text-to-speech program enables the writers to hear their text as they write it. At the simplest level the teacher could program in a selection of phrases for a student to use to retell a known story. At a higher level the student can type in the words or select them from a word bank.

Collaborative approaches

Literacy Through Symbols (Detheridge and Detheridge 2002) provides many examples of creative writing produced with the help of symbols and computer software.

The student can have a grid of key vocabulary but the teacher or classroom assistant is on hand to type in additional vocabulary. Pupils can also work in groups, using interactive whiteboards so that pupils can all see the screen and take part in writing the story.

Telling a story

George, a non-speaking six-year-old, used software that allowed him to indicate certain words or pictures. A number of screens were prepared each with pictures. George could select pictures using a switch, so that as the story unfolded he could choose what happened next, or in which direction the story would go.

The simplest story involved an imaginary journey. The first screen had different vehicles to indicate how they were to travel, other screens had places, items, activities or characters. The story-teller – the teacher – responded to George's selections at the appropriate time and incorporated them into the narrative. Over time the stories became longer and more complex, as both the narrator and the student became more familiar with the technique.

Dictation

Writing through dictation, where the student expresses the ideas and the teacher puts them down on paper, is an important stage in building confidence in writing. The 'writing' can be traditional orthography, symbols, drawings, or a mixture of all three.

Fiona Grey used the anthology *Caribbean Dozen*, edited by John Agard, as the inspiration for writing poetry with students with severe learning difficulties at St Ann's School, Merton. First, the students studied the poems, looking at the language and illustrating them. They then dictated their own poems, either in speech, sign or both. Once they were written down, the poems were read back to the students, to see if they wanted to change anything. Care was taken to build up the students' perceptions that they were going to write poems, and that their language was going to be valued as much as the words on the printed page.

The students' poems were submitted to the Merton Young Poets competition and published in the anthology *Hear My Voice*. Students attended the presentation at the Town Hall and received certificates, which were framed and displayed in school. The students had a real sense of accomplishment. One boy, when asked about himself by his new teacher, was proud to tell her that he had had a poem published.

Stimulating writing

Structured activities

For students who have little confidence in writing, carefully structured activities can provide a safe 'way in'. Stories or poems, or other students' writing, can be the basis for such activities. Before starting any writing, students need to be familiar with the text. Use symbols to support the writing as appropriate. Read it to them, read it with them, then let them read it alone. Ask them questions about the story, the plot and the characters.

Structured writing activities based on familiar texts

Cloze procedure. Write simple sentences from the story with key words missing. Students can choose the missing words from a separate sheet, and cut and stick them in place.

What's wrong? Re-write a part of the story with some key words in silly places. Students can read the story and cross out the wrongly placed words.

Give students a copy of the story. Ask them to change the story by changing some words or even whole lines.

Cut the story into sentences, or write key events on separate strips of paper. Ask students to put them in the correct sequence.

Use the story as a spelling exercise by leaving blank any words students are learning, for them to fill in.

Remove the initial sounds of key words, so that students can write them in.

Produce the story in book form, for the student to illustrate.

Story frameworks

Word banks and overlays can be used to support emergent writing (see pages 60–2). Start by familiarising the students with a basic story line, for example a journey, a picnic, a trip to the park. Then retell the story, leaving gaps for them to fill with their own inventions, either by speaking, signing, writing or using symbols. As they become more confident, leave progressively larger and larger slots for them to fill. The scripts that provide the frameworks can be programmed onto communication aids, and then onto overlays or grids for writing.

Frameworks can be used in a variety of ways:

- *Round robins*: Each student has one part of a story programmed on to an aid, and the story unfolds as each person contributes. Students can also read their contributions from symbol scripts.

- *Story comments*: Tell or read the story. Stop at key points and invite students to comment, or select comments programmed onto communication aids. At first, pre-select suitable responses so that all choices are correct. For example, if at one point in the story a lion enters, suitable responses may be 'Help', 'Roar', 'Run', 'Hello Lion'. Once students are familiar with the techniques, they can select and use their own ideas.

When the stories have been created orally, they can be written down (using symbols if appropriate) by the students themselves or a helper. A tape recorder or video (to record signs or gestures) provides an invaluable record of the session.

Story scripts or frames

Use a conventional script for a story outline. Students can slot in their own elements.

1. **A dark dark night**

   It was a dark dark night
   Alice and Jarwed and Sharon were sitting at home, **when suddenly**
   There was a knock on the door
   Who is knocking on the door?
   Alice opened the door
   Nobody there!
   Alice went out to look

   It was a dark dark night
   Jarwed and Sharon were sitting at home, **when suddenly**
   There was a knock on the door
   Who is knocking on the door?
   Jarwed opened the door
   Nobody there!
   Jarwed went out to look

   It was a dark dark night
   Sharon was sitting at home, **when suddenly**
   There was a knock on the door
   Who is knocking on the door?
   Sharon opened the door
   Nobody there!
   Sharon went out to look

   It was a dark dark night
   Where is Alice?
   Where is Jarwed?
   Where is Sharon?
   Who is knocking on the door?
   You say!

In this story frame, the scripts are programmed onto communication aids. The three named students perform the actions as the storyteller narrates. The final denouement is decided by the group – and might change each week.

Figure 5.5 Some examples of story framing

Consequences

This game has a simple framework:

a person . . .
went somewhere . . .
met someone . . .
did something . . .
and the consequence was.

Students can contribute at each stage to create a story.

---

2. Consequences

a person . . . went somewhere . . . met someone . . . did something . . . and the consequence was . . .

This story frame was used with a group of three students with moderate/severe learning difficulties, using their own preferences for activities and stars. For the final sequence, they dressed up in the appropriate gear and had their photographs taken. The results were made into books for them. The students had to select their alternatives from magazine pictures, and also decide which activities were appropriate for each student.

Dave	Anna	Richard
went	**went**	**went**
to Arsenal	to a disco	to a club
met	**met**	**met**
Tony Adams	Take That	James Bond
scored a goal	**danced** all night	**played** cards
and then . . .	and then . . .	and then . . .
won the cup	**went** to Bermuda	**got** the girl

Figure 5.6 Some examples of story framing

Building a framework

Start at the same point each lesson, with the same sentences, and develop it further each time.

3. I woke up one morning

I woke up one morning

I went downstairs

and I saw...

snow/a lion/a feast/a flood

act out what happens next

then write about it.

This story frame was used week by week, first using only one activity until the students were familiar with it, then building on the students' own imagination.

Figure 5.7 Some examples of story framing

Group writing

For students who are getting started on the process of writing, collaboration can build confidence and generate ideas. Many of the ideas discussed already in this chapter involve students working in groups.

Students can use many different ways to communicate their ideas, for example photographs, cuttings or symbols. As part of the activities associated with *The Hound of the Baskervilles* at Coppice School (see page 47), pupils worked on the anonymous letter sent to Sir Henry Baskerville, using the time-honoured technique of cutting out individual words and letters from a newspaper. Pupils then created their own letters, or simply cut out the letters for their names.

Creating poetry using overlays

At Cheyne School for pupils with physical disabilities, Helen Cockerill, the speech therapist, ran a poem group each week with a group of five- and six-year-olds. The children were provided with a strong framework, using concept keyboard overlays with Bliss symbols (one of the systems used with people who have cerebral palsy and find it difficult to access traditional orthography) to support choices, with grammatical colour coding. Eventually this led to more creative output.

The children used the overlay shown below to contribute lines to this poem.

CHOCOLATE FEET AND STICKY HANDS

by Jodie, Daniel and Adam

I want cold feet.
I want sticky hands.
I want!

I don't want chocolate feet.
I don't want lots of hands.
I don't want!

You and me don't want sticky hands.
You and me don't want lots of feet.

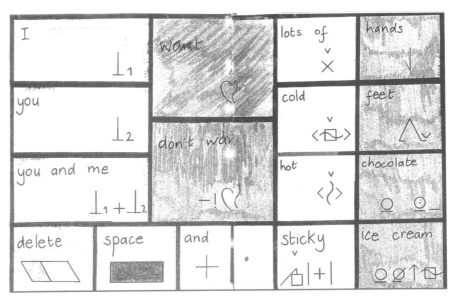

Figure 5.8 Concept keyboard overlay for 'Chocolate Feet and Sticky Hands'

Group writing with dictation

Students at Heathermount School for autistic pupils created a poem after a workshop on *Macbeth*. The seven boys in the group built up the poem through fragments of what they remembered from the text and the associated activities

Donald, who started and finished the poem, is a silent boy who generally finds it very difficult to participate in groups and stay on task.

The students' sense of achievement as they each came up to read out the poem created one of those magic moments that keeps you going as a teacher, despite the pressures of paperwork and inspections.

How shall we start our poem?

Donald: Hubble, bubble, toilet trouble
Fire burn and cauldron bubble.
Night noises
Anthony: As Macbeth walks through.
Vampires.
Donald: Ha ha ha.
Anthony: Screeching doors screech here and there.
Peter: There's an owl
Too-whit too-whoo
Anthony: Macbeth draws closer.
As wolves howl.
Peter: Wind
Blows and whistles, whew.
As Macbeth is killing sleep.
Anthony: Macbeth is king and here comes trouble.
Donald: Knock on the door! Move it on the double!

So the finished poem looks like this:

Hubble, bubble, toil and trouble
Fire burn and cauldron bubble.
Night noises as Macbeth walks through.
Vampires – ha ha ha
Screeching doors screech here and there
There's an owl – too-whit too-whoo
Macbeth draws closer
As wolves howl.
Wind blows and whistles, whew.
As Macbeth is killing sleep.
Macbeth is king, and here comes trouble.
Knock on the door! Move it on the double!
Hubble, bubble, toil and trouble
Fire burn and cauldron bubble.

Figure 5.9 Macbeth poem, by Heathermount School pupils. Words in italics were contributed by staff

Video and photographs

Because video and television are so much a part of students' lives, they can provide a familiar and valued way of starting stories. For example, one group of secondary students with learning difficulties wrote a story based on an incident in a 'soap'. They then acted the story, taking photographs of the key scenes. These pictures were scanned into the computer and dialogue added in speech bubbles. The resulting comic strip book was creative, interesting and well presented, giving a real feeling of self-esteem to the authors.

> Ted Hasslebring from Vanderbilt University (in the US) used video as a basis for storytelling and writing with a group of students with learning difficulties.
>
> First the students watched a cartoon with their teachers and parents, to become familiar with the events. Stills from the video were then printed to give them reminders and tools for retelling.
>
> The students sequenced the action, using the stills as cues for telling the story.
>
> Next they used the same video images on a computer to provide the illustrations for their own re-writing of the story.
>
> Finally they were encouraged to write a new story using some of the stills if they wanted, but changing some aspects of the original.
>
> The structured approach slowly built confidence, and let the students face one new challenge at a time.

Starting with objects

For students who have profound learning disabilities, and cannot use either text or symbols, it can be difficult to know what creative writing might mean. However, you can engage them in a group writing activity by encouraging them to choose objects as a prompt for the writing of the rest of the group. For example, Myles Pilling has used memory objects at Rainbow School in Kent. An object associated with a particular event is brought in for a 'Show and tell' session with the group and used as the basis for discussion – is it old or new? What is it for? What story can we make up about it?

> A pupil's grandfather gave him an old World War I helmet with a dent in it, which stimulated some of the group to think and write about it, while the role of the pupil with profound disabilities was to be the centre of attention, holding the helmet.

Presenting students' writing

Once students have completed a piece of writing, it is important to show how much it is valued. Create a wall display for individual pieces. Books can be made from students' handwritten work or by printing out words or symbols on a computer. Students can illustrate these themselves, or choose photographs or pictures from magazines, clip art or other sources to accompany the text. Small format books can be made from folded paper. A4-sized pages can be put into individual plastic wallets in a ring binder.

Students can take their writing home to share, and share it with others in school. They can read their own stories and poems aloud or in a group.

Ryan's book

Ryan, who has moderate learning difficulties, attends a mainstream school. His story about a lion who lost his mane is full of imagination. He dictated his story to his support worker, who typed it for him, enabling him to follow the flow of his ideas and demonstrate his creativity. Using the symbols as well as written words helped him to identify the meaning of the words he couldn't read.

Ryan then illustrated the story and it was put together into a book. This made his work look professional, conferred additional status and showed that it was valued, which in turn increased his self-esteem and confidence. Having completed this story, Ryan was enthusiastic about writing rather than it being a formidable task.

Figure 5.10 Ryan's story (reprinted from Detheridge and Detheridge 1997)

CHAPTER 6
Developing storytellers

I wish, my dear sister and my Lord the King, that there were more time to tell you also the story of the Fisherman and the Brass Bottle, for it is really much better and more wonderful than this tale ...

Queen Sharazad saved herself from the threat of execution each dawn by engrossing her husband with tales of the Arabian Nights.

(Amabel Williams Ellis, *The Tale of Queen Sharazad*)

N, a seven-year-old Pushto speaker, had been identified as a slow learner with language difficulties. She ended a retelling in Pushto of Quentin Blake's *Patrick* with the sentence 'And that is the ending', which the interpreter identified as a traditional form of story conclusion (Campion 1997). Although she had significant problems in learning, N had picked up an important skill that allowed her to take part appropriately in a valued activity.

As we saw in Chapter 1, the sharing of stories lies at the heart of our social and linguistic identity, and there is plenty of evidence to suggest that children's narratives reveal their knowledge of cultural experiences and conventions (McCabe and Bliss 2003). Knowing how to frame stories is important for social inclusion, and is also critical to the development of language and literacy (Snow 1983). Research has shown that children are often able to produce more complex language in the context of storytelling than in conversation (Milosky 1987).

In educational contexts, children are faced with the tasks of talking about their experiences and what they have read or seen, whether in Science, History or English. Narrative recall is prominent among the skills demanded by the English National Curriculum, and is required in both Speaking and Listening and in Writing. The skills involved in narrative are not only cognitive (recall and sequencing) and linguistic (the mastery of structures for connecting clauses), but specific and conventional. In the example given, N had learned how a story should be told in a particular social context.

Storytelling is becoming increasingly recognised as a valued form of communication. The ability to construct narratives is closely associated with successful learning and achievement for pupils – probably because it is a demanding activity which requires children to coordinate a number of different skills simultaneously. Therefore, if you can tell a story you are likely to be good at other academic tasks (Bishop and Edmondson 1987; Paul and Smith 1993). And storytelling is also vital for children's social and emotional development.

This chapter focuses on oral storytelling skills.

What is a story?

There are many different ways of deciding what counts as a story, and how you decide to teach or support children in storytelling depends to a large extent on your definition. At first this seems easy – a story has a beginning, middle and end; characters; and things that happen. One model of storytelling that is often used in teaching insists that the events of the story must conform to a particular structure. This is referred to as a 'story grammar'.

Story grammar

Stories are seen as composed of logical sequences of information (statements) organised into episodes. After providing a setting (such as introducing the character), the story is composed of problem-solving episodes.

Basically, something happens to characters, which causes them to respond to it or to set up a goal. Their actions or their attempts to accomplish the goal result in some resolution or state of affairs that terminates the episode. Episodes may follow one another sequentially or be embedded in other episodes (Stein and Albro 1997).

The problem with this narrow definition is that it rules out an awful lot of storytelling behaviour. In fact, this approach is derived from an analysis of classic European folk tales, and has been shown to be inappropriate for the analysis of storytelling from other cultures, and of conversational and personal anecdotes told by both children and adults (McCabe and Bliss 2003). In the story grammar model, children only start to be credited with true narrative when they have a language age of four to five; this excludes many students with communication and language difficulties. So we need some definitions that are broader and more inclusive.

The one-word story

Teacher Vivien Paley makes regular use of storytelling in her class and has a special area and time for students to tell stories. Everyone gets the opportunity to do so, and the class often respond by acting out another student's story. She describes one particular student who had learning difficulties and very little verbal communication, who stood up at story time and said one word: 'Mummy'. That was taken as his story, and his classmates proceeded to act it out for him, taking the roles of the family and interacting with him.

In contrast to the story grammar framework, which demands a high level of cognitive performance, this approach suggests that almost any behaviour can potentially count as a story, depending on the social context and the way in which it is framed. For students with special educational needs, as for younger children, a broad approach to storytelling is most useful.

> **Story involves telling another person about a real or imagined event**

A mature story consists of:

- structural elements (the characters and the plot, opening and closing phrases)
- affective, emotional elements (ways of telling the story which help the listener to engage with it)
- social strategies for checking audience attention and response
- rhetorical aspects and use of language.

There is an example of a story analysed using this framework in Appendix 4.

Table 6.1 Aspects of storytelling

Structural	Emotional	Social	Rhetorical
Introductions and *closures* to the story	*Verbal aspects:* reference to feelings, thoughts and motivations of characters	*Ways of getting listeners to attend:* Hey, listen!	Use of figurative language (metaphor and simile)
Orientation (who, when, where information)	*Non-verbal aspects:* stress, pausing, pitch, volume of voice, facial expression and body movement	*Checking and monitoring listener reactions:* (Yes? You know?)	*Well-known sayings:* (Went like clockwork; You could have knocked me down with a feather)
Sequences of actions		*Responding to listeners' feedback*	
Climax or 'high point' of the story			*Repetition for effect:* (first we went... then we went... then we went...)
Resolution: how the story ends			*Use of formulae and conventions:* (on and on; time and again)

Children's storytelling

Children seem to begin telling stories very early indeed. Early narratives have the character of 'scripts', recalling what usually happens in generalised events (Nelson 1986). Between the ages of two and three, children begin to recount personal events, provide on-line commentaries to narrate the events in their play, and tell fictional stories (Allen *et al.* 1994; Fox 1993; Hicks 1990). William's stories (below) illustrate how sophisticated a three-year-old's narrative can be, especially when supported by props in context, or when elaborating a very well-established tale.

> Amazon, aged 14 months, saying what happened the day before when she went on an outing:
>
> Baby
> Hester
> buggy
> drink
> balloon

Examples of storytelling by William, aged three years two months.

Script: getting your hair cut
I go on the bus and walk to the haircut shop and I play in the big toy car and put my apron on and then I have my hair cut and then the lady does my hair and dry it and you go home again and change shoes.

Personal narrative
At nursery a man came with a big camera and I talked to him and he was Gordon.
(William's nursery was used as the photo opportunity for a well-known politician.)

Commentary (playing with Spiderman and Action Man dolls)
He kill that bad lady in the house he did
The bad lady is gone
And he couldn't catch the bad and he couldn't and action man couldn't catch the bad lady in the forest he couldn't
He's just lying down for the doctor
He's just lying down for he's lying down
The action man is waiting for the doctor to make him better cause a different one hurt him
He hurt his tummy and his head
He had to wait for the doctor
Here comes the ambulance (nee naw nee naw nee naw)
Now the other doctor come in the ambulance
Untintelligible sounds while apparently 'fixing' man.

He's all better now

Well-known fictional story: *The Grufalo*
There was a deep dark wood
The mouse was walking in the deep dark forest
Saw a fox from the deep dark wood
The mouse saw the fox and the mouse looked good
Where are you going to little brown mouse?
I going to have lunch with a Grufalo
Then there was a grufalo
Do you know?
His tongue is scary

Storytelling skills

Age 1–2 years

Children begin to make reference to past events, and can participate in narrative with adult help. First they just label an event – for example, 'gone', which adults will expand: 'Oh, you dropped your teddy. Where did it go?' Once children can put two words together they begin to produce longer sequences of narrative which are ordered in time, that is they correctly state what happened first, then what happened next. For example: 'Dropped my cup. Broken.'

Age 3–4 years

Children begin to use structural components, usually referring to one or more events. By around $3\frac{1}{2}$ they are able to tell you where something happened, but are less good at saying who was there. Three-year-olds link their narratives with 'chains' such as 'and then', and tend not to use complex constructions such as 'because', 'when', 'before', though they seem to be aware of why things happened and the need to provide an explanation. By age 4, however, most children are using a wide range of conjunctions to link their statements. Four-year-olds are more likely to include introductions to the narrative, but are likely to get the order of events in a complex narrative mixed up, often starting with the climax of the story and working backwards.

Age 5–7 years

Children regularly tell the listener where and when the story happened and who was involved. They begin to organise stories around a central event. During this period, children make their understanding of character and psychological understanding more explicit; they understand the basic emotions, the intentions of characters and stock characteristics of fictional characters such as heroes and villains. By age 6, children can produce complete structured narratives. As they get older, understanding of the relationships between characters and context becomes more sophisticated. They show recognition of the need to provide explanations for events and behaviour; complex emotions such as guilt and jealousy, and understanding of different time frames (days, weeks, years, long ago). They make explicit their insights into the difference between appearance and reality (for example, the witch is pretending to be nice, but she wants to eat Hansel and Gretel). Their own stories become more elaborate, with multiple episodes and sub-plots, and reflecting more than one point of view.

Age 8–10 years

Children show reflective skills – the ability to think about their story as a story and discuss themes, characters, differences of interpretation and the way they are telling the story. By the age of 10, most children are able to tell complex stories which are structurally coherent, and which are adapted to the needs of different audiences

Later development

Narrative skills continue to develop in childhood, and the number of complete episodes increases up to the age of about 16. It is obvious that adults can also develop their storytelling abilities by learning from others, such as skilled practitioners. In cultures that value storytelling, this is more common than in our society.

Storytelling by students with special needs

It is only fairly recently that an interest has been shown in narrative production by people with different types of developmental disabilities. Young people with special needs of varying levels of severity can produce narratives, but their ability to organise all the details will differ.

- Students with language delays and difficulties tend to have problems with recalling and organising information (Loveland and Tunali 1993; Miranda *et al*. 1998).
- Students with Down's syndrome tend to perform at the level of their mental rather than chronological age. They can include details about people in the story, but they often seem to miss the main point and include irrelevant information (Reilly *et al*. 1990; Fabbretti *et al*. 1997).
- Students with autism can link events into a sequence but often they miss the main point of the story, and its emotional significance (Goldman 2002; Loveland and Tunali 1993; Norbury and Bishop 2003).

However, we should be wary of making too many predictions on the basis of categories of special need, or level of ability. Little comparative data is available from special populations, and relatively little attention has been paid to how narrative skills might be taught to children with more severe disabilities, whose language abilities are limited. Because feeling is carried through intonation, stress, gesture and facial expression, and because features of a story can be conveyed through mime, it is in fact possible to tell an engrossing story with very little verbal language.

Students with learning difficulties can frequently recall isolated aspects of an event or story, but lack the skills and experience to construct a sequence. However, with appropriate intervention, it appears that both typically developing children, and those who have learning difficulties can improve their ability to tell stories (Hemphill *et al*. 1994). Moreover,

Andreas, a man with moderate learning difficulties, no speech, and gross use of gesture, provided a vivid account of how he was mugged on a bus, using space to show where he was sitting and how the man approached him, and intense and emphatic gestures, vocalisation and expressions to convey his feelings.

the contexts in which stories are elicited, the materials used, and the type of story required all have an effect on the extent to which children deploy their skills

The effect of context on styles of storytelling

You need to think about what kind of story you want the child to tell, and how best to prompt and support the storytelling, before you start. It is no good concluding that the child never uses the past tense if you are only ever asking for an account of what usually happens. Equally, you should not conclude that they are using only single words and not linking the events, if you are sitting next to them and pointing to a sequence of pictures.

Types of story

> Primary school children asked to produce an ongoing film commentary, news report and a story recalled from memory used more emotional language in the story, and the least causal language in the ongoing commentary.

- *Scripts and routines* (about what usually happens): Present tense, use of 'you', events that are linked, but little reference to characters and intentions.
- *Personal narratives* (about things that happened to the individual): More description, more single complete episodes. Use of past tense.
- *Fictional narratives* (imaginary stories, stories read or seen): More multiple and incomplete episodes, more action sequences. Use of past tense.

Stimuli

Video or moving images stimulate stories with fuller references to characters and more dynamic gestures and actions than do still pictures. Children telling stories from their own imagination use more advanced narrative structures than those relying on pictures, where they are likely to describe what they see. Still pictures are probably the most commonly used, but the least successful, stimulus for oral narrative.

The listener

Children tell more complex and complete stories if they believe that the listener does not know the story already. The worst situation for storytelling is where you are both looking at a set of pictures and the student knows that you know the story. This is true for both typically developing children and those with learning difficulties. On the other hand, shared experiences enable adults to give much better support through prompting than when they do not know what the child is talking about – so a balance needs to be struck. It is often helpful for an adult who does know the story to support the child in telling it to another adult who is new to it.

Prompting and supporting storytelling

Since the ability to tell a complete mature narrative independently emerges slowly, through plenty of practice with supportive adult listeners, you also need to take account of the stage at which students are functioning, and provide intervention that is appropriate to each level.

There are three basic principles or requirements for storytelling to happen with all students, from the most to the least able.

> The three basic requirements for storytelling are:
>
> Experience
> Opportunity
> Audience

- *Experience:* The starting point for narrative is that there must be something interesting happening in students' lives before they will want to tell a story about it. This may seem obvious, but when I collected stories from parents and teachers of children and adults with profound learning difficulties, I was surprised how few were personal narratives or fictional stories – most were accounts of what usually happens on holiday or during the week (scripts) and likes and dislikes. So if we want our students to tell stories, we have to make sure there is something to tell a story about.

- *Opportunity:* Once there is an experience to share, there must be the opportunity to do so. There need to be many different kinds of opportunity – from the standard news or circle time at the beginning of the day, to planned assemblies or performances, to a multiplicity of spontaneous small stories of recent events that are shared with just one or two friends or teachers. This means that some thought needs to be given to managing the timetable to facilitate this.

- *Audience:* Once the opportunity is taken up, there has to be a culture of supportive listening – not just by adults but by the whole class and school. Children need to learn not only how to tell stories, but how to listen.

Strategies that encourage narrative

Modelling – tell the student a story yourself: 'Once I had this awful injection...' and then ask for a similar personal experience from them.

Topic extensions – those which help the student to follow up his own narrative: What happened then? How did you feel?

Repetition – 'You fell down?' with expectant intonation.

Expansions – repeating what the student says and adding further information – 'You fell down, and you hurt your knee!'

Verbal attention – show that you are attending keenly, with feedback and reactions, positive engagement.

Clarifying questions – directing the student to provide orientations and evaluations.

Persistence – keep prompting the student to participate in the dialogue, by offering your own contributions, responding to what she says.

Prompts for unshared experience – a genuine motivation for the student to tell.

Information-rich feedback – you add new information to help the child remember.

Strategies that discourage narrative

Topic switching – going on to a different topic when the child still has something to say, perhaps because you cannot get the drift of the story.

Over-use of closed or specific questions, which turn the interaction into an interrogation.

Inattention – seems obvious, but showing you are not interested is a big turn-off.

Direct correction – 'No, we didn't go to the café, say we went to granny's.'

Prompts for shared experience – 'Go on, tell daddy what we did on the way home from school'.

Repetitious feedback – with no expansion.

(McCabe and Peterson 1991)

Storytelling at different developmental stages

Pre-verbal level

This group includes children with severe language delays who have not yet started to talk or use signs, and students of all ages with profound and multiple disabilities. Stories need to be very short and quite ritualised, with the character of rhymes and music. Your aim is to help the student to pay attention to the story and to join in. Call and response narratives, where one person leads and the audience responds at particular points in the story, can be very successful, using both fictional and personal stories.

At an individual level, students may benefit from the experience of sharing 'scrapbook stories' (see page 82). Communication aids and musical instruments can be used to help students participate. However severe the disability, all students should have an opportunity to take centre stage and tell their own stories. This becomes extremely important at times of transition, where students need to have some access to the shared memory of people, places and things that they are leaving behind.

For good examples of life story books or communication passports used in this way, see Gray and Ridden 1999; Middleton and Hewitt 1999.

Call and response

Keith Park uses this extensively with pupils who have profound and multiple disabilities, with the more verbal students calling out the lines.

Excerpt from his Cinderella

> Say hello to Cinderella (Hallo Cinderella)
> Cinderella's ugly sisters (Booo!)
> They were off to a Three Day Party (Oooh!)
> Where the Prince might find a bride (Aaah!)
> Can I come? Said Cinderella
>
> They said:
> You can't go, cos you can't dance
> (You can't go, cos you can't dance)
> You can't go, you've got no clothes
> (You can't go, cos you can't dance)

Example of a personal story – Dinah's Glasses

Based on an actual event, where Dinah was looking for her glasses, this story was told repeatedly to a group of people with profound disabilities, using a voice output communication aid for the refrains.

> Dinah's looking for her glasses
> (Dinah's looking for her glasses)
> Where've they gone?
> (Where've they gone?)
>
> Under the table? (Nooo!)
> On the TV? (Nooo!)
> In her bag? (Nooo!)
> In comes Joe, says 'Whose are these?'
> (All together) They're Dinah's!

Early language level

As students begin to develop language, they will benefit from many opportunities to join in telling stories, although they may take a long time to do so independently. Useful strategies for this group include the following.

Group telling

In work at the Bridge School, we found that students really benefited from telling well-known stories all together. We made up little tales about things that really happened, as well as fictional events, and once we had constructed the story and acted out, we re-told it as a group all together. This gave students a lot of confidence.

Contextual supports

- providing a model of how to do it (tell an exemplar story; watch Sesame Street News Reports)

- providing brief picture prompts (for example, photos of significant events)
- providing a story book cover and pages with minimal prompts, or blanks, which invite the child to act a storyteller
- puppet audience or stooges who have to have a story explained to them
- providing scripted 'lead-ins' ('Once upon a time...'; 'I was walking down the road when...')
- providing prompts ('What happened next? And then?')

The aim at this stage is for the student to supply the main 'stepping stones' of the narrative, while you fill in the gaps. This keeps the story-telling 'balloon' in continuous motion, and avoids the trap of asking too many questions, which turns it into an interview, not a story.

Two ways of telling a story

Question and answer

So, what did we do yesterday?
Park
Yes, we went to the park. And who did we see there?
Jim
That's right, your friend Jim. And who was with him?
Dog
Yes, and what did it do?
Poo

Gap filling

Something really disgusting happened yesterday! We went to the...
Park...
And we saw...
Jim
And Jim had his...
Dog
And the dog did a...
Poo

Although the difference may seem slight, in the gap-filling method you have two narrators collaborating to tell a story, whereas the question and answer method is more like an inquisition.

Scrapbook storytelling

It is often difficult to have a 'real' conversation with students whose language skills are very limited. You may find yourself asking 'dead-end' questions (based on what you know has been written in the home–school book), which are no fun for either of you.

'Did you go to the shops?' 'Yes.'

'And what did you buy?' No response. (Student can't remember, or doesn't have the word/sign/symbol available.)

'Did you buy an ice-cream?' 'No.' etc.

Carolyn Musselwhite is a teacher and researcher in the field of augmentative communication. She suggests another successful way of eliciting narratives from students whose language skills are limited, or who are using communication books and charts. Scrapbook storytelling offers a way of communicating about events that is more creative, through collecting mementoes, and using 'multiple choice' alternatives. These need to be used in quite a formal way at first, to teach the student how to do it.

Using scrapbook storytelling

By making an individual scrapbook for a student, you help them to remember and tell a story of an experience.

Making the scrapbook

Materials: Durable book, such as a mini photo album.

Mementoes:

Outings (paper hat from café; church bulletin; 'dead' balloon from party).

Events (lock of hair from haircut; price tag from new shoes; speeding ticket incurred by mum).

Simple pictures, symbols and line drawings can also be used to trigger memories about events, or to look forward to them. For example, a picture of a trampoline from a catalogue.

Set up:

On the first page write instructions on how to use the book with the particular student. For students with severe physical handicap it is essential to describe their means of indicating a response, including any consistent gestures, signs, or vocalisations.

Stick a memento on one page. On the facing page write two or three relevant questions, with alternative answers next to them in symbol or picture form. Leave space on the page for an information box where you can write in any new information/comments from the student, more details about an outing, etc.

Training

For students who have little memory of events, and relate mostly to events in the present, you will need to go through the 'story' and help them make the connections. For example:

What's this?

Hat

Where did we go?

(On the page there are symbols for the alternatives: café, garden, swimming pool. Point to hat and then to café symbol).

What did we eat?

(Alternatives: *banana, burger, biscuit*. Point to *burger.*)

Conversation training

A sequenced training approach, gradually introducing more people, seems to be the most useful way of getting the book used regularly.

1. Practising the routine. You model the question and then answer for the student (you could use a puppet).
   'Where did you get the hat?'
   Then go round to the student's side, and answer the question – or prompt her/him to do so.
2. Introduce a third person. Try to leave the student to work through the activity; prompt if needed.
3. The third person brings in another person, for example a visitor or a member of staff from another room.

Later language levels

As students become more competent at telling narratives independently, you can reduce the amount of support, while remaining a responsive listener. Once students can give a sequence of events, are confident that they can tell something new to an audience, and have had plenty of modelling in how to introduce and structure a narrative, they will be able to benefit from more specific prompts.

> More specific activities for children with relatively advanced verbal skills can be found in:
> Hayward and Schneider 2000; McCabe and Bliss 2003; Roth and Spekman 1984; Shanks 2003.

- *Who? What? Where?*
  You can use games and prompts to elicit information about the setting, making sure the children include the information needed to start the story off. For example, Becky Shanks suggests using colour-coded cards to remind students to say who was involved, and where and when the story happened.
- *Sequencing*
  Games and prompts can help children sequence events correctly. They can organise the information, first using their own written sentences or pictures and then retelling the story from memory. You or a puppet can make deliberate mistakes in a sequence for them to correct.
- *Genre differences*
  Help the children to differentiate types of story by making explicit reference and categorising. 'It's a story about me and my friends', 'It's

a fairy story', 'It's a news story'. This will sensitise them to the kinds of language and style of telling that are appropriate.

Autistic spectrum disorders

Children with autism are likely to find storytelling very challenging, mostly because of the need to engage with the audience's perspective, but also because of the level of imagination, reference to feelings and intentions of others demanded. Carol Gray is a researcher working in the field of autism, who has devised social stories, based on the concept of scripts. These are personalised accounts created with students, which are designed to help them make sense of and predict the experiences they are likely to encounter and that they find difficult.

Social stories

These seek to provide scripts that autistic people may need to know in order to interact appropriately with others. Four types of sentences are used:

Descriptive – describes what people do in social situations.
People usually stand in line at the bus stop. When the bus comes they get on one by one. They give their money to the driver and sit down on a seat. If there is no seat, they stand.

Directive – states what the desired behaviour is.
I come to the bus stop. I stand behind the other people who have got there before me. When the bus comes, I wait for these people to get on first. Then I get on and give money to the driver.

Perspective – presents the reactions of others to situations.
People sometimes get cross if the bus does not come on time. People are pleased when the bus comes.

Control – identifies strategies that the person can use to help remember and understand.
I remember that I have to stand in line by thinking of the rows of seats in the bus.

For specific guidelines on writing social stories, see Carol Gray's website (details in Appendix 3).

Personal narratives

Social stories are essentially accounts of routines. They differ from personal narratives and from fictional stories, which usually involve a departure from the routine – the experience becomes a story precisely because it is something different and not predictable.

Can students learn to tell personal narratives?

In a small research project in 2004, Estelle Keen investigated whether autistic children would benefit from teaching in how to tell personal stories about unique events.

The child was asked to tell two stories, using a 'story stem' approach, where the researcher provided brief prompts such as 'Once I hurt my arm and had to go to the doctor. Has anything like that ever happened to you? Yes? Tell me about it.'

The child then selected one of the stories to work on every day for a week. Each day, for about 20 minutes, the researcher built up and expanded the story with the child, and practised telling it. The child drew and wrote in a book outside that period, but the emphasis was on face-to-face storytelling. After a week the child was re-tested on both stories, and six weeks later on the original story.

All the children showed improvements in narrative structure as a result of the intervention, which were carried over to the follow up – although the stories that had not been practised did not improve.

The theory behind this research is that over time, personal narratives become very practised and rehearsed – we tend to recycle anecdotes and memorise the script for them. This means that the children could use their (rather good) rote memories to construct some basic stories to share with others.

However, the children benefited in different ways from the intervention. Some of them really enjoyed acting out their own stories and recalled the dramatic effects, whereas for others this was too much and they needed a low-key approach. In some cases, although the second narrative was more complete, the first had a fresh, spontaneous quality which evaporated over the rehearsal period. In this respect, the children were no different from the rest of us – the thirtieth time we tell our funny story is rarely as engaging as the first!

Fictional narratives

Children with autism can also engage in fictional narratives.

Wolves

Isaac is a pupil attending a special school for children with autistic spectrum disorders. He dictated this story about wolves to his teacher.

'I like the safari park. I see lots of animals. I saw some wolves. They look like me. They eat bones, your bones! If we were out there, getting out, the wolves would eat our bones. They would hunt, they'd crunch and rip your top. I can smell the bones. I can smell wolves. I hear the howls' (makes loud wolf howl).

In their book *Developing Drama and Play for Children with Autistic Spectrum Disorders*, Sherratt and Peter demonstrate that students with autistic spectrum disorders can engage in sustained narrative play, if the appropriate support is provided. They suggest using a very structured approach called 'prescribed drama structures', so that the student becomes familiar with a framework, which is gradually modified to become more imaginative and less predictable. They provide many examples of children whose play became more flexible and less ritualistic once they had practised in this kind of context.

Prescribed drama structures

This is a ritualised activity that resembles a game with a clearly defined beginning, middle and end.

One actor is always in character role, and the children learn the practice of make-believe through learning to play the game in a rule-based way. The key elements of the approach are:

- Sense of play – the teacher emphasises that this is play and pretend, not real.

- Fastness of rules – the teacher agrees some rules with the children, for example about where the acting space is and what you do in it.

- Accepting roles and symbols as part of the rule of the game, before necessarily 'believing' in them. The teacher does not attempt to explain what it means to pretend to be a character; she just encourages the children to copy her in role.

- Modifying actions in the light of the make-believe; you can change something that happens during the play – for example, Cinderella's dress might have to change from red to blue because that's what the fairy godmother says must happen.

Storytelling is a skill that emerges from experience in particular cultural contexts. Children are socialised into storytelling by what they hear and see.

Students with special needs can be helped to develop their narrative skills by the provision of appropriate prompts and contextual support, but what is vital is to provide a culture of expectation, by offering them continual opportunities for recalling and reconstructing events. Everyday events such as outings, playground incidents, surprises and accidents need to be seized on and retold, perhaps at the end of the day with a wall chart or symbol timetable. In this way, students become familiar with their own stories and those of others. In so doing, they build up a sense of who they are and the communities in which they live.

CHAPTER 7

A framework for evaluating students' responses to literature

'But there is something – not an Ology at all – that your father has missed, or forgotten, Louisa. I don't know what it is. I have often sat with Sissy near me and thought about it. I shall never get its name now. But your father may...'

'Where are the graces of my soul? Where are the sentiments of my heart? What have you done, O father, what have you done, with the garden that should have bloomed once, in this great wilderness here?'

(Charles Dickens, *Hard Times*)

Within the National Curriculum, considerable emphasis is placed on assessment of student responses, using hierarchical level descriptors that are criterion-referenced. The current framework uses a developmental approach (the P-scales, or Pre-Level 1 Scales) to profile the attainments of students with special educational needs from the earliest stages of learning (P1–3) to Levels 1–3 of the National Curriculum, the levels at which typically developing children can be expected to function in their first years at school.

This chapter discusses the role of evaluation in the context of an arts-based approach to the teaching of literature, and presents a framework for evaluation that allows teachers to consider the quality of a student's response from different perspectives. An illustration of the framework in practice is given on page 92.

This framework is not referenced to key stages and levels of attainment. This is because we really have no evidence as yet about levels of development in 'affective intelligence' (Goleman 1996) or 'intelligent sensing' (Ross 1978). Most of the work which has been done on key stage assessment in literature, or text comprehension in the National Literacy Strategy, relates to achievements in written language, located within the cognitive domain. The levels of attainment set out in the curriculum documentation make some reference to feeling states, using terms such as 'lively', 'imaginative' and 'confident', but they are scattered randomly across levels, and there appears to be no logic in the gradations from one level to another. Rather than attempting to grade responses to literature, the approach outlined here relies on detailed description of how students communicate their reactions to an experience. These descriptions are appropriate to students from P1 onwards, and allow for small, spontaneous responses to be taken into account.

The purpose of assessment

Assessment may be undertaken for a variety of reasons:

- *diagnostic* – to identify learning strengths and weaknesses
- *summative* – to provide an absolute indication of a level of achievement
- *comparative* – to compare one pupil with another, in order to ascertain levels of achievement
- *formative* – to assist the process of teaching
- *evaluative* – to monitor the effectiveness of teaching.

There are clearly areas of overlap between each of these categories. The purposes of assessment of response to literature are essentially *formative* and *evaluative*, for both student and teacher.

Assessment contributes to the process of profiling students' achievements, by illustrating the contexts and the forms through which they can respond in ways that are discriminating, creative and affective. It allows teachers to monitor and evaluate their work, and to see what the experience means to the people they are teaching. Essentially, we are interested to know the effects on our students of the texts we use and the way we present them. Are we communicating what we thought we were communicating? Is the approach working? Does it stimulate their abilities to think and feel and express themselves?

'Reading what is happening' suggests an ongoing, dynamic, descriptive process in which we are continually trying out an approach, observing its effects and adapting what we do. From this point on, the term 'evaluation' is preferred to assessment because it suggests an orientation to the process rather than the product.

> ...all teaching involves responding appropriately to what students do and say. And responding appropriately suggests that we can in a sense 'read' what is happening.
> (From 'Assessing musical Quality in the National Curriculum', K. Swanwick)

Evaluation

The first step is to clarify why we want to evaluate, and the type of evaluation that is appropriate. Since the purpose is to inform our own teaching, and to contribute to our knowledge of the potential of our students, the evaluation should be richly descriptive of the student's response, rather than a test that the student must pass or fail.

To see how students respond to the experiences we offer them, we need to observe and evaluate all the ways in which they show reactions.

This includes not only written output or oral narratives, but also their body language, the way they use their voices, their gestures and their facial expressions, paintings, drawings, movement, dance and song. When asked how they evaluate pupils' reactions, teachers of students with special needs invariably mention these behaviours. These are the signals that combine to provide us with information about the student's expressive response to literature.

The evaluation framework on page 93 is based on the following principles:

- A concern with the development of aesthetic responses grounded in feeling and sensation, through which distinct ideas and reflective cognition may evolve.

- A view of literature as a social and cultural experience, as well as private and individualised. Students' participation and understanding grow through repeated exposure to conventional forms in contexts that support their learning.

- A view of meaning as a product of the creative interaction between the student and the text, rather than inherent in the text, and accessible only to those who can crack the code. This does not imply that any and all interpretations of a text will be valid, but allows us to look at what interactions and meanings are possible for particular groups of students, and to acknowledge that people's experiences of a text are likely to differ. What interests us is the relationship between the writer's product, the response of the individual, and the impact this has on a cultural community.

The expressive response

The expressive response is defined as 'that which represents or symbolises feeling' and is the basis of the arts curriculum (Ross 1978). The starting point is a *sensation*, which gives rise to *feeling*, which may be transformed into an image (visual, auditory, tactile, smell or taste) that the mind works on and considers – Do I like it? What does it remind me of? Is it the same as or different from another experience? Is it a surprise? What was just a sensation becomes a *perceptive idea*, or insight, as it is integrated into the frameworks that we use for understanding and judging what is going on around us. This is a largely unconscious process. Once we consciously explore the experience, we have moved to the stage of *reflection*, where we actively think or talk about what it means to us. In most texts concerned with the assessment of artistic responses, the assumption is that the student then progresses to *creative output*, usually by articulating a personal response. This could take the form of imaginative or critical writing, but could also be a drawing, a piece of music, or a dance. It is the student's *creative output* that is normally the focus of attention.

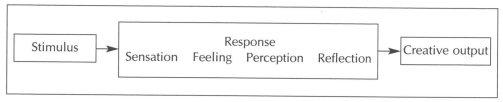

Figure 7.1 The response continuum

However, many students with special needs will not be able to produce anything material or performance-based. If we want to evaluate the effect of the experience, we must find a way of describing their immediate expressive responses – how they show us that they have engaged with the text. We do not have to depend on an output to look at their potential for creativity.

Student responses

Reactive expression is behaviour that simply releases or gives vent to feeling, and is about the discharge of tension.

Creative expression is about feelings changing and growing – controlled, deliberate responses that give form to feeling. (Ross 1978)

So, we present our students with an experience, and they respond to it in whatever way they can. At first, they may only respond reactively, but even this is valuable as a starting point. The forms that their immediate response will take will vary, but will always consist of some kind of physical, behavioural signal that we 'read' (see box below). Creative output originates in the physical and imaginative responses that result from the student's engagement with the experience.

Modes of expressive response

Immediate personal response

- Body orientation (tense, relaxed, turned towards or away, slumped or upright, etc.).
- Facial expression.
- Vocalisation.
- Use of the hands (reach, touch, throw, pull, push, etc.).
- Movement.
- Gestures that represent objects and events.

- Signs from a sign language (British Sign Language, Paget-Gorman Signed Speech, Makaton Vocabulary).
- Spoken words.

Transforming response into creative output

- Writing: forms
  Using conventional text.
  Using graphic symbols such as Rebus, Makaton, Picture Communication Symbols.
- Visual and plastic arts
  Drawing, painting, collage, sculpture, textiles.
- Music
  Singing, using instruments.
- Dance
  Choreographed movement.
- Drama
  Dramatic production.

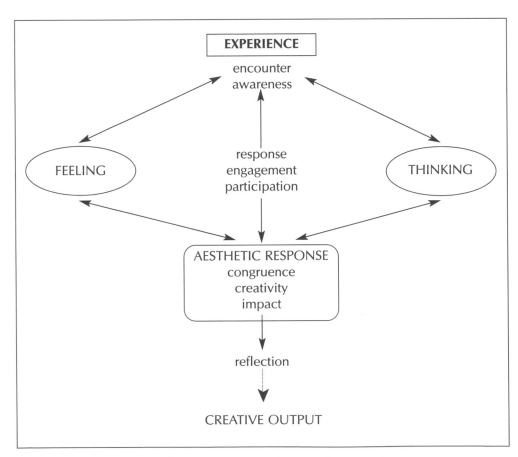

Figure 7.2 Response to literature: an evaluative framework

Framework for evaluating response to literature

How we read students' responses – how we interpret what they mean – depends on what we are looking for. The framework for evaluation presented here focuses on four perspectives for evaluating an expressive response:

- *experiential* (engagement/attention)
- *affective* (feeling)
- *cognitive* (thinking and language)
- *aesthetic* (unity of engagement, thinking and feeling).

Experiential

Since some level of engagement or attention is a prerequisite to the development of a response, we begin by evaluating the level of the student's reaction to the experience. This involves focusing on the level of the student's engagement with the activity – are they attending, enjoying and involved with the lesson? Brown's hierarchical model of levels of experience (see below) is widely used to assess students' involvement and learning potential.

Levels of experience

- *Encounter* – being present, being provided with sensations.
- *Awareness* – noticing that something is going on.
- *Response* – showing surprise, enjoyment, dissatisfaction.
- *Engagement* – directed attention; focused looking, listening; showing interest, recognition, recall.
- *Participation* – supported participation, sharing, turn-taking.
- *Involvement* – active participation, reaching out, joining in, commenting.
- *Achievement* – gaining, consolidating, practising skills, knowledge, concepts.

(from *Religious Education for All*, E. Brown)

In relation to the response continuum on page 91:
- *encounter and awareness* probably operate at the level of *sensation, response, engagement*
- *participation and involvement* represent a stage at which *perceptions* or *ideas* may be developing
- *achievement* is the point at which *reflection* would probably develop.

Affective

Affect concerns the level and the quality of feelings that the student expresses in response to the experience. 'Level' is used to indicate the extent to which students are able to enter into the experiences of others, engage with them, and grow emotionally in so doing. From studies of affective development we know that infants at first react to the emotions of others, which may begin as a purely imitative behavioural response.

However, the imitation of an expression may be enough to generate the associated feeling (see page 5). From about two years onwards, children acquire and use words to express feelings (like, love, happy, sad), and they not only make associations between predictable events and feelings (for example, birthdays and pleasure) but seem to understand that other people have feelings that differ from their own. By four years of age, children recognise the mental states and feelings of other people (Baron-Cohen 1993).

Levels of affect

In this framework for evaluating responses to literature, there are four levels of development for affective responses:

- *Reaction* – immediate affective response to atmosphere or sensation (laughter and excitement in the battle scene of *Macbeth*, unease with spooky music).
- *Imitation* – showing response to the feelings of others (imitating someone else's facial expression, joining in with vocalisations).
- *Empathy* – showing some response or awareness of the feelings of others (a comment, reaching out to touch someone who is acting (or really) sad).
- *Imaginative empathy* – ability to take on a role (imagining what someone else (fictional or real) would feel like).

As well as having some idea of the level of response, we need to evaluate the quality of response at each level. Students may not be able to talk or write in ways that directly convey their feelings. Here we are concerned more with the quality of the feeling, its range, intensity and appropriateness, however it is expressed.

Quality of feelings

- *Range* – how many different feelings can the student express in different contexts?
- *Intensity* – how involved does the student become in the imaginative experience?
- *Appropriateness* – does the emotion expressed fit with the context? For example, some students may not get beyond the stage of laughing to express release of tension at the most dramatic moments, but others may be able to control their expressions of mood to suit the atmosphere.

Table 7.1 Ways of looking at affective responses

	QUALITY		
	Range	Intensity	Appropriateness
LEVEL			
Reaction			
Imitation			
Empathy			
Imaginative empathy			

Enjoyment

One of the most common questions that teachers ask students is: 'Did you like the story/poem/film?' The purpose of asking it is not always evident, since we do not necessarily have to like an experience (or like everything about an experience) in order to get something out of it. However, this can be a starting point for exploring with the student *what* they liked (or not) and *why*. For students with more severe learning difficulties, if they do not enjoy the experience at some level, they may not attend, and therefore are unlikely to learn anything – hence it is important to record evidence of likes and dislikes.

We generally rely on reading facial expressions and body language to determine enjoyment or dislike, so if you are working with people who have multiple disabilities, you may mistakenly interpret involuntary facial movements, such as grins or blinks, as indicative of feelings. However, the responses of some students may be very individual, so that only people who know them well can determine how they felt about the experience.

To establish preferences for events, objects and activities, the usual approach is to present two items that are equally familiar. The one that is chosen consistently over time is probably the one the student likes. Preferences will also be indicated by the extent to which a student is willing to tolerate, or actively join in an activity.

Cognitive

This is concerned with the students' conceptual and linguistic response to the experience. The framework for evaluation draws on the National Curriculum, as well as theories of the development of language functions (Roth and Spekman 1984).

We need to evaluate the student's ability to recall, predict, explain, justify, compare and contrast; in other words, in memory (recognition and discrimination) and thinking skills, and the way these are expressed in language.

Recognition

The starting point is the student's capacity to recognise similarities and differences, since this appears to be fundamental to the way in which infants categorise and attach meaning to experience (Mandler 1992).

To establish whether or not students recognise and remember the experience, you can observe their discrimination, anticipation, choice of correct object of reference, moving to habitual place, looking at or picking up an associated object when a piece of music is played as a cue.

Thinking skills

The key thinking skills are involved in accessing all areas of the curriculum. These are most evident in students' linguistic responses (spoken, signed or written), but they may also be demonstrated non-verbally, for example when students solve experimental problems by actually manipulating materials, or in the composition of a piece of music. The way that students interact with others may indicate that they are predicting what will happen next, or understand a problem in the context of a story.

> **Thinking skills across the curriculum**
>
> - Describing, comparing and contrasting.
> - Predicting.
> - Recall and sequencing.
> - Hypothesising and imagining.
> - Problem-solving.
> - Reasoning.
> - Instructing.
> - Debating.

Language skills

The framework of the English curriculum emphasises the teaching and assessment of students' abilities to understand and express themselves linguistically.

The key aspects are:

- *vocabulary and meanings* – the range of concepts available to a student, and the relationships between sets of concepts (antonyms and synonyms; categories of words such as fruit or furniture)
- *grammar* – the structure of words and sentences
- *pragmatics* – the appreciation of the way in which language use varies with context.

These can be assessed using the P-scales or language assessments (Knowles and Masidlover 1982; Locke 1985; Latham and Miles 2001).

I was able to infer that Susan, a woman with profound learning difficulties, remembered a drama session when, in response to being shown the case for the video cassette we used, she took it, got up and moved to the room where we held the session.

Aesthetic

Although aesthetic judgements are both relative and subjective, there is general agreement that aesthetics is concerned with the fitness of form to purpose, artistic creativity, and cultural relevance. The aesthetic aspect of a response is concerned with the integrity of form, thought and feeling in a cultural context. In evaluating the aesthetic quality of a student's response, we can focus on three key aspects:

- *Congruence*

  Does the response fit with the context in a way that is satisfying or apt? This is a slightly different concept from appropriateness of feeling, which is more to do with social acceptability. Here the aptness lies in the relationship between the form of the student's response and the meaning of the text.

- *Creativity*

  Defined in this context as innovation. Does the student's response add anything new to the experience?

- *Impact*

  The effect of a student's response on the rest of the group. Does it contribute in a way that affects the social context? This relates to Geertz's idea that art is not perceived in isolation, but is part of a network of social and cultural interactions.

Lenny

Lenny, a stocky young man with Down's syndrome, communicated primarily non-verbally, although he had a small vocabulary of manual signs, which he occasionally combined in two-word sentences. He took part each week in a dramatisation of the *Odyssey* through interactive games.

One activity involved the nymph, Calypso's, desertion by Odysseus, and involved a paired dance where Odysseus slid his hands down the arms of his partner until only fingertips were touching, before turning away. This activity was designed for people with dual sensory impairment, in the knowledge that loss of a familiar and trusted partner is an all-too-familiar occurrence in institutions where staff turnover is high, and leaving rituals are often perfunctory. The dance was envisaged as slow, sad and sexy, to blues music.

However, for Lenny the meaning seemed to be different. He was dancing with a staff member whom he rather fancied, and he introduced a sort of twirl as he turned, and a little wave, which was distinctly flirtatious. It had the effect of changing the atmosphere by injecting a note of humour.

Odyssey Now, Nicola Grove and Keith Park.

The example of Lenny illustrates what is meant by impact. Lenny's response was not congruent with the atmosphere that we were trying to establish. However, he was contributing his own meaning in a way that did not just affect himself and his partner, but had an impact on the group. Therefore, we can evaluate his behaviour not only for an integrity between form and feeling (which was undoubtedly present) but for a social dimension: the extent to which it contributed to the framing of meaning for the group.

Intentionality

A question that is particularly relevant for students with profound learning difficulties, is whether a response needs to be intentionally produced in order to qualify under the heading of aesthetic evaluation. Because our approach defines meaning as something that emerges as the product of an interaction, it allows for the contribution of unintentional, 'serendipitous' responses from students to the creative atmosphere of the event.

The following examples of unintended responses were observed during projects which focused on Shakespeare's *Macbeth* in schools for pupils with severe and moderate learning difficulties.

Shezad

Shezad has profound and multiple learning difficulties, with no verbal communication. For most of the time his realisation of the role of King Duncan was characterised by its half-heartedness. He would lean his chin on his hand, crown sliding over his ear, and stare into the middle distance, unmoved by the devotion of his followers, the battles waged on his behalf, and the wiles of his hostess. However, for some reason, Shezad came to life during the game which dramatised the Macbeths' choice between good and evil, loyal friendship and murder. This involved each actor confronting Shezad, and being pulled towards a dagger (to the left), or a chalice (to the right), by staff who alternated lines from the play supporting one position or the other: 'He's here in double trust' (pull to right); 'When you durst do it, then you were a man' (pull to left).

Shezad is hemiplegic, and can only raise his right hand to reach or point, although I had forgotten this when setting the game up. But when Shezad suddenly started shouting loudly and pointing to the right side each time someone was confronted with the choice, I realised that his limited motor skills were being employed to considerable dramatic effect.

Jenny

Jenny also has profound learning difficulties, but was much more engaged in the drama than Shezad. She has no functional hand skills at all, and we monitored her involvement principally by checking her gaze direction and facial expression. She did, however, vocalise, and at the point where we were developing character through various exercises (music and vocalisation), she seemed to imitate a wail for Lady Macbeth by a high-pitched, prolonged vocalisation.

Nadia

Nadia's role was Lady Macbeth. Mostly she had to be supported to stand or move, and she rarely made eye contact with anyone, although she frequently smiled. Nadia has Rett's syndrome, a genetic condition which affects cognitive, communicative and motor functioning. One of the most characteristic features of Rett's is obsessive clasping and re-clasping of the hands, often known as hand-washing. Now, 'hand-washing' in Rett's syndrome may not usually be functional (indeed we spend a lot of time trying to substitute more positive alternatives) but the character of Lady Macbeth offers the perfect opportunity to endow this behaviour with meaning, albeit in a very limited way.

This example may be seen as controversial; in fact one arts worker with whom I discussed this approach thought it was highly irresponsible. I offer it because I think it makes for an interesting debate about our responses to disability. We might decide that the risk of reinforcing maladaptive behaviour was too great. Or we might decide that since we can never totally eradicate the behaviour, this is one context where it will be accepted.

In each of these three examples, behaviour that is unintentionally produced by the student is endowed with meaning in the context. We use 'scaffolding' to frame and contextualise the student's response, just as we do in the development of communication with infants and people functioning at a pre-verbal level (Nind and Hewett 1994; Coupe and Goldbart 1988), or in the development of creative writing. At an aesthetic level, the behaviours are congruent with the atmosphere of the play.

The next examples are of students with rather more linguistic ability, who were able to involve themselves actively in the drama.

Gail

In the scene immediately before Macbeth's murder of Duncan, the students were asked to supply spooky noises that might be heard at night. Groups of students came up with different ideas – a creaky door; an owl hoot; the wind. Gail had been behaving in a very autistic way during the workshop, wandering across the acting space, twiddling obsessively and apparently failing to notice anything that was going on. However, when her group were asked to volunteer a sound, Gail looked me straight in the eye and produced an eerie 'Miaow'. Needless to say, this was the sound adopted for their contribution. Gail's contribution was not only congruent, but also creative – she was adding a new element within the framework of the game.

Stephen

Two scenes on, the murder had been carried out, and Macbeth and Lady Macbeth were frantically washing their hands. I was narrating along the lines of 'They had to try to get their hands clean, when SUDDENLY...' I paused fractionally, and Stephen, a student with moderate learning difficulties, without any prompting interjected three loud, peremptory knocks on the bench beside him. Stephen knew the story, since the students had been told it, had watched the video, and had made props before the workshop. His response showed not only that he could recall and sequence the events of the story, but that he could also produce a dramatic effect which was aesthetically congruent.

Stephen was not really innovating – he was reproducing something he had heard and seen in the correct place in the story. But he enhanced the meaning and raised the general level of engagement of the group. In that sense, he made a powerful impact on the social context of the interaction. There was no doubt that the rest of the audience really responded to his action.

The framework for evaluation in practice

As an illustration of how the model might operate, let us work through the example of Jenny's 'Lady Macbeth wail'.

Experience

Observation of Jenny's behaviour suggested that she was definitely *engaged* for most of the session, since she watched what was going on, smiled and produced excited vocalisations.

Her *participation* had to be supported by Eddie, the assistant who was holding her throughout, but the fact that her cry immediately followed on from my model suggests that she may have been echoing it.

Affect

Jenny's vocalisations, as stated, seemed to convey mainly excitement. She can express pain and discomfort, and pleasure through low vocalisations at other points. She has little control of facial muscles, and although we tend to interpret her smile as indicating enjoyment, it may at times be reflex. Her wail, however, had a distinctly melancholy quality to it. In subsequent sessions, therefore, we might look to see if we can get Jenny to reproduce this quality (we might also play with different sounds in a music session). In terms of the level of expression of affect, Jenny seems to be functioning mainly *reactively*, although she may be able to *imitate*.

Cognitive

Jenny is operating at a pre-verbal level, and mainly reacts to stimuli, though she does at times show evidence of anticipation. Her contingent vocalisation suggests the potential for imitation. We might want to see if in subsequent sessions when we are working with Lady Macbeth's sound, Jenny can reproduce her cry, or introduce it spontaneously.

Aesthetics

The sound Jenny produced definitely showed *congruence*: it was appropriate to the atmosphere, and to the character. Although it may represent a new departure for Jenny, it was an imitation rather than an *innovation*. As far as the *impact* goes, it was not clear whether the other students were aware of the quality of the sound, although I picked up on it and commented. We would want to see if subsequently Jenny's sound could help to build a social meaning for the group which conveyed something of the character of Lady Macbeth.

Using the framework for evaluation

The framework for evaluating students' expressive response focuses on four areas:

- the level at which the student engages with the experience;
- the feelings the student expresses;
- the thinking and language processes that are evident;
- the aesthetic dimension of the response (the quality of the form of the response and its social implications).

This approach offers a way of thinking coherently about behaviours that we often recognise to be exciting, or unexpected, or spontaneous, but that we can only note as anecdotes in the absence of a structured framework. If we cannot define what is significant about these behaviours, there is a risk that they will be undervalued and ignored, particularly in the current outcome-obsessed climate.

> . . . such people usually attempt only to assess those aspects of education which seem to lend themselves to precise measurement, and that other aspects become victims of what might be called the 'disappearance by default' syndrome – the notion that what can't be measured doesn't exist – and vanish in a kind of educational 'Bermuda Triangle'!
> (E. Goodman, in *Assessment and Education in the Arts*)

The framework may be applied in various ways:

- To contribute to a profile of students, by describing their affective and creative potential.

- As a basis for developing some form of creative output – dance, drama, artwork, music or writing. The framework provides continuity between students who can only respond expressively, and those who can move into creative production. It also allows for continuity between creative arts subjects in the curriculum.

- To support progression for individual pupils. By focusing on key aspects of their responses, we may enable them to develop a greater range or depth of engagement, feeling and aesthetic contribution.

- As a way of capturing the significance of responses by people with profound learning difficulties, which are often fleeting and intermittent.

There is no need to work through all aspects of the framework for every student. It is up to the teacher to decide what is important to evaluate for particular students in particular lessons. For example, you may want to focus on the way a student uses language in different lessons – so the focus would be on the cognitive dimension. Or you may only want to get a measure of the student's level of engagement, in which case you could look at the levels of experience.

Other frameworks will also be useful. For example, if the student's response is primarily through dance, art or music, you could use the assessment tools recommended in the relevant National Curriculum documents, and other texts in the *Curriculum for All* series, such as *Music for All* (Wills and Peter 1995); *Drama for All* (Peter 1994); *Art for All* (Peter 1996); and *Dance for All* (Allen and Coley 1996).

1 Examples of poetry styles

Simple language

Language which can be readily understood, with simple sentence construction and a lot of basic vocabulary.

Grace Nichols, *Sea Timeless*

H. H. Munro, *Overheard on a Salt Marsh*

Charles Causley, *What Has Happened to Lulu?*

Robert Frost, *Stopping by Woods on a Snowy Evening*

Anon., *This Is the Key of the Kingdom*.

> What has happened to Lulu, mother?
> What has happened to Lu?
> There's nothing in her bed but an old rag doll
> And by its side a shoe.
> (from *What Has Happened to Lulu?*, Charles Causley)

This simple poem is full of suggested meanings, but the vocabulary is well within the grasp of a pupil who has a basic range of signs and words.

The poem can be built up with question and answer, putting some of the lines on a Big Mack, and by creating a 'set' of the room – the open window, doll and shoe, which can be named by the children.

At fifteen I went to the army
At fourscore I came home.
On the way I met a man from the village,
I asked him who there was at home.
'That over there is your house,
All covered over with trees and bushes.'
Rabbits had run in at the dog hole,
Pheasants flew down from the beams of the roof.
In the courtyard was growing wild grain;
And by the well, some wild mallows.
I'll boil the grain and make porridge,
I'll pick the mallows and make soup.
Soup and porridge are both cooked,
But there is no one to eat them with.
I went out and looked towards the east,
While tears fell and wetted my clothes.
(*Old Poem*, translated from the Chinese by Arthur Waley)

I know I am always going on about using the original text and not paraphrasing, but that doesn't mean you can't tinker a little bit for the benefit of students. For this poem, if I felt the students could not manage *pheasant* and *dog hole*, I would be strongly tempted to substitute *bird* and *cat flap*, or just *door*. I think I would also use *nettles* rather than *mallows*, not least because we could then actually make soup and porridge and thus create the sensory experience of the poem.

Concreteness

Descriptive language referring to sensory experiences which can be illustrated by real examples or pictures.

John Keats, *The Eve of St Agnes*
Adrian Mitchell, *Giving Potatoes*
e.e.cummings, *maggie and molly and milly and may*
James Berry, *Sunny Market Song*
Mary Hoberman, *Yellow Butter*
Christina Rossetti, *Goblin Market*
William Carlos Williams, *This Is Just To Say*
Maya Angelou, *Woman Work*

What wondrous life is this I lead?
Ripe apples drop about my head
The luscious clusters of the vine
Into my mouth do crush their wine
The nectarine and curious peach
Into my hands themselves do reach
Stumbling on melons, as I pass,
Ensnared by flowers, I fall on grass.

(from *The Garden*, Andrew Marvell)

You do not need to know that Marvell is punning on a version of the Garden of Eden and that the poem is about Platonic ideas of the soul and the imagination, to enjoy the sensuous imagery. It is but a short step to creating the garden in your classroom, complete with piles of mown grass (use green cloth for students with allergies), ripe apples falling (just avoid the students' heads), nectarines, peaches and grapes. You may not be able to go as far as the wine, but you can subsitute grape juice. Contrast this ripe sensuality by illustrating what follows (as the mind withdraws into solitude) using a quiet period of flute music with a silver bird mobile, made by the children themselves.

Had I the heaven's embroidered cloths,
Enwrought with golden and silver light,
The blue and the dim and the dark cloths
Of night and light and the half-light,
I would spread the cloth under your feet:
But I, being poor, have only my dreams;
Tread softly, for you tread on my dreams.

(*He Wishes for the Cloths of Heaven*, W. B. Yeats)

Opportunities here for textile art – create the cloths of heaven in the class with paint or appliqué on blue cloth. Study the night sky (slides and photos) go to planetarium, make pictures and then go and choose the right material from a big warehouse together – sari lengths with silver thread come to mind. Use this like a parachute, walk on it with bare feet, then take the cloth away and imagine the dreams instead. Each child thinks of a dream, paints or appliqués something to represent it, puts this on the wall and then you create the imaginary stepping stones that must be walked across. All this even before you get to the love interest – an entire term's work.

Rhythm and sound

Language which is strongly patterned, conveying meaning through sound and sense. 'Onomatopoeia' is the technical term for words with in-built sound effects (e.g. 'moo', 'splat', 'tee-hee', 'pitter-patter'). This poetry can be readily illustrated by sounds or music, using contrasts between vowels and consonants; short sounds and long sounds; hard sounds and soft sounds.

Anon., *The Ballad of Casey Jones*
Alfred Tennyson, *The Lotus-Eaters; The Splendour Falls on Castle Walls*
Hilaire Belloc, *Tarantella*
John Masefield, *Cargoes*
Kit Wright, *Red Boots On*
James Berry, *Diggin Sing*
T. S. Eliot, *Skimbleshanks the Railway Cat*
W. H. Auden, *Night Mail*
Eleanor Farjeon, *Cat*

> The Assyrian came down like a wolf on the fold
> And his cohorts were gleaming in purple and gold
> The sheen of their spears was like stars on the sea
> When the blue waves roll nightly on deep Galilee.
> (from *The Destruction of Sennacherib*, Lord Byron)

> This dramatic poem is full of the sound of the thundering hooves, with a strong rhythm that can be beaten out on a drum – try one group doing it in four beats while another does it in 12, and contrast the loud parts of the poem with the quiet of defeat and mourning. Charge up and down the hall in wheelchairs.

> Downward through the evening twilight,
> In the days that are forgotten,
> In the unremembered ages,
> From the full moon fell Nokomis,
> Fell the beautiful Nokomis,
> She a wife but not a mother.
> She was sporting with her women
> Swinging in a swing of grapevines
> When her rival, the rejected,
> Full of jealousy and hatred
> Cut the leafy swing asunder,
> Cut in twain the twisted grapevines,
> And Nokomis fell affrighted
> Downward through the evening twilight,

On the Muskoday, the meadow,
On the prairie full of blossoms.
'See! A star falls!' said the people
'From the sky a star is falling!'
(from *Hiawatha*, Henry Wadsworth Longfellow)

The mesmeric rhythm comes from the *Kalevala*, the great Finnish epic, which Longfellow encountered in a German translation. The *Kalevala* is traditionally recited through the night in a dance, or by two narrators taking hands and rocking back and forth, and you can do *Hiawatha* in the same way. Start with establishing the rhythm, and gradually the sense of the story will emerge. (Note that you now have another use for grapevines.) Beware – after working on an adaptation of parts of the *Kalevala* myself (for a visit to Finland), I drove my family mad by issuing instructions and composing shopping lists along the lines of *When you get your schoolthings ready/don't forget to take the text books/or your teachers may be angry/as you promised to return them*, etc.

Repetition

Language which builds up meaning through repeated sequences and refrains (e.g. traditional folk and fairy tales, songs and ballads).

Anon., *The Strange Guest*
Dylan Thomas, *Do Not Go Gentle into that Good Night*
Anon., *Lord Randal*
Edward Lear, *The Jumblies*

Will you come?
Will you come?
Will you ride
So late
At my side?
Oh will you come?

Will you come?
Will you come
If the night
Has a moon
Full and bright?
Oh, will you come?

Would you come?
Would you come
If the noon

Gave light,
Not the moon?
Beautiful, would you come?

Would you have come?
Would you have come
Without scorning,
Had it been
Still morning?
Beloved, would you have come?

If you come
Haste and come.
Owls have cried;
It grows dark
To ride.
Beloved, beautiful, come.
                              (*Will You Come?*, Edward Thomas)

This lovely simple poem gains its urgency from the repeated request. Does she ever get there? You can make up the story and complete the poem with a verse starting 'When you came...'

Hot sun, cool fire, tempered with sweet air,
Black shade, fair nurse, shadow my white hair.
Shine, sun, burn, fire; breathe, air and ease me;
Black shade, fair nurse, shroud me and please me.
Shadow, my sweet nurse, keep me from burning,
Make not my glad cause cause of mourning.
Let not my beauty's fire
Inflame unstaid desire,
Nor pierce any bright eye
That wandereth lightly.
                       (from the play *David and Bethsabe*, George Peele)

This poem also comes under the heading 'Sensory images and rhythm', but to me the first impression is of being flooded with the same words over and over again, in their different combinations, like a complicated song. It has to be one of the sexiest poems in the English language, but all of that is in the inferencing, which need not be at all explicit to your pupils. There is a gorgeous painting by Rembrandt of Bathsheba bathing (with the nurse behind her) as she reads the letter from King David informing her that her husband has been killed in the front line (which the King arranged in order to have her as one of his wives); you could use this as an illustration.

Dramatic language

Language which conveys character or narrative and can be illustrated through acting, exaggerated for emphasis.

Robert Browning, *The Pied Piper of Hamelin*
Samuel Taylor Coleridge, *Rime of the Ancient Mariner*
Vachel Lindsay, *Daniel Jazz*
Anon., *The Ballad of Frankie and Johnnie*
Lord Macauley, *The Keeper of the Bridge*
W. H. Auden, *The Quarry*
Mike Rosen, *Hot Food; The Chocolate Cake*
W. B. Yeats, *The Cap and Bells*

> Gr-r-r there go, my heart's abhorrence!
> Water your damned flowerpots, do!
> If hate killed men, Brother Lawrence,
> God's blood, would not mine kill you!
> What? Your myrtle bush wants trimming?
> Oh, that rose has prior claims-
> Needs its leaden vase filled brimming?
> Hell dry you up with its flames!
> (from *Soliloquy in a Spanish Cloister*, Robert Browning)
>
> Perhaps the most eloquent poem ever written about how living in close proximity with people can drive you to murder – it is actually very funny. What on earth has the poor man done to inspire such loathing? You don't have to understand any of the words if this is declaimed in the right tone of suppressed fury and sarcasm. This is a great poem for using to talk about how to deal with anger and our feelings for other people. Follow it with something equally dramatic but more positive in feeling such as:
>
> Sir Brian had a battle axe with great big knobs on
> He went among the villagers and blipped them on the head.
> On Tuesdays and on Saturdays (but mostly on the latter days)
> He knocked at all the cottage doors, and this is what he said.
> 'I am Sir Brian (take this)
> I am Sir Brian (take that)
> I am Sir Brian as bold as a lion
> Take that and that and that'.
> (from *Bad Sir Brian Botany*, A. A. Milne)

Oh, I forbid you, maidens all
That wear gold in your hair
To come or go by Carterhaugh
For young Tam Lin is there.

There's none that goes by Carterhaugh
But they leave him a pledge
Or else their ring or mantle green
Or else their maidenhead.

Janet has tied her kirtle green
A bit above her knee
And she has snooded her yellow hair
A bit above her bree
And she is off to Carterhaugh
As fast as go can she . . .

(from *Tam Lin*, traditional ballad)

This poem can be dramatised into a short play, giving pupils roles
and dialogue and creating scenic effects.

More ideas for using poetry across the range of ability can be found in
the resources for pupils with special needs on the Poetry Society website,
www.poetrysociety.org.uk.

APPENDIX 2 Principles of translation into graphic symbols and signs

Tina Detheridge and Nicola Grove

Symbols are graphic representations for ideas, objects or actions. They have been used as part of written communication systems for centuries – Egyptian hieroglyphs are perhaps the best known. We use symbols in our environment today to convey meaning efficiently and quickly, avoiding the need to read complex text: for example, road signs, symbols on the iron to show the steam position, symbols on seed packets to show if they need full or partial sun.

For many years, symbols have been used to support people with communication difficulties as a means of letting others know what they want (such as pictures for a drink or TV). More recently, they have been used to help non-text readers become literate. The following sections provide a brief overview of symbols and the issues surrounding their use, as a means for accessing literature, and as a tool for helping non-text writers become authors.

There is a range of ways of representing information in graphic form. At one end of the spectrum are pictures. These are fine for representing simple concrete ideas (car, hamburger, traffic light) but it is not so easy to convey more complex or abstract information (independence, meeting, dream).

In the middle range of the spectrum are pictorial symbols, normally simple line drawings, created to represent single ideas or concepts, and at the far end of the spectrum are abstract symbols, which have a logic that governs the way they are constructed. Bliss symbols, for example, are made up of different elements which when put together create new meanings. For example, compare the pictorial (Rebus) symbol for 'trousers', which is a line drawing, and the Bliss symbol for the same thing:

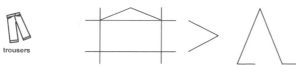

Figure A2.1 Rebus trousers, Bliss symbolics trousers

The Bliss symbol is a compound made up of the symbol for cloth, the symbol for goes and the symbol for legs, and it's obviously much more complex than the Rebus symbol. People with learning difficulties are more likely to recognise and remember the pictorial symbol than the abstract symbol.

Relationship between meaning and symbol

There are several pitfalls when using pictorial symbols, which need careful thought if the relationship between the image and the meaning is to work well. In some cases, you can translate each word to a symbol quite easily:

Figure A2.2

However, sometimes you have a choice of symbols for one word, and it is important to select the right one.

Figure A2.3 Two ways of representing 'back'

Here the picture of a person's back confuses the meaning rather than enhances it, and you need the second type, which is time-related.

Conventions for symbols

Some pictorial symbols are also constructed using logical principles. You will notice that the pictures for the following places all use the outline of a building.

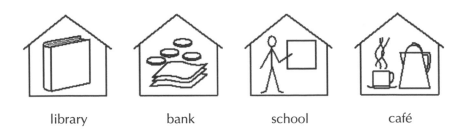

Figure A2.4 Symbols for different buildings

There are other schematic structures in the vocabulary, for example in time and space. Consider these alternatives, which clearly show the conceptual differences between words that are the same.

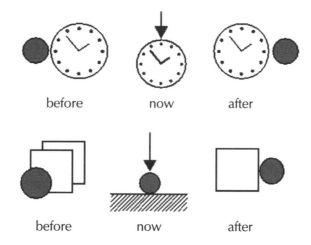

Figure A2.5 Symbols showing time and space relationships

Other symbols represent meaning by combining elements, rather in the way that Bliss symbols do. Try and identify the combinations in the following symbols.

plumber   animals   great   confident

Figure A2.6 Compound symbols

Other words are difficult to convey in pictures – for example: if, but, sorry, but, is. These can only be represented by fairly arbitrary abstract symbols, which are difficult to recognise and recall.

Presentation

The relationship between text and symbol should ideally be considered for each individual reader. Issues to consider include how many symbols to use, and the relative size of text and graphics.

Some pupils may be able to cope with reading an exact word-to-symbol version, whereas for others it may be easier just to symbolise key words, omitting all the small linking words.

Readers who can recognise some text may benefit from a display with large text and small symbols, whereas readers who are mainly relying on the symbols may want large symbols and small font text.

Translating literary text into symbols

Texts vary in the extent to which they can be translated literally. Consider the two poems represented below.

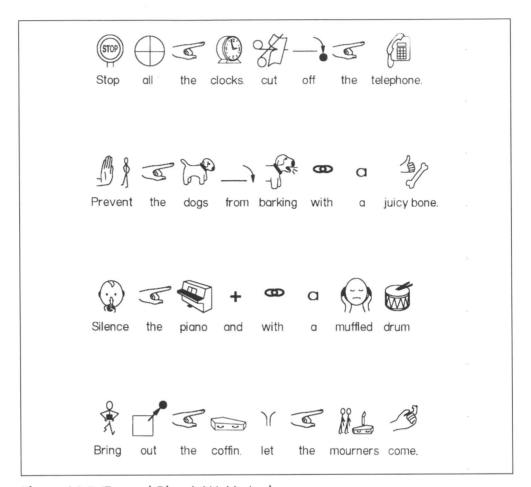

Figure A2.7 'Funeral Blues', W. H. Auden

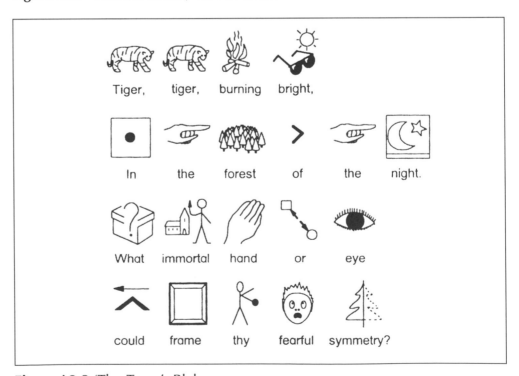

Figure A2.8 'The Tyger', Blake

The Auden poem has very straightforward concepts which can be represented quite easily by the pictorial symbols, whereas the concepts in the last two lines of the Blake poem are very difficult and do not lend themselves so easily to visual representations.

There is a very particular problem with poetry, which is an aural medium. If the words on the page are prompts for the sound of the words, it can be argued that the symbols also need to prompt the sound rather than the conceptual meaning. A typical example is the word 'before' in the following quote from *Macbeth*. Normally 'before' has a time-based meaning, but Shakespeare uses it in a spatial sense:

Is this a dagger I see before me?

Figure A2.9

This is not the correct interpretation of the word 'before'. There may be an alternative word in the vocabulary already linked to this image. If not, it is possible to add the word 'before' to the symbol for 'in front'.

Is this a dagger I see before me?

Figure A2.10

Both of these versions are now technically correct. However, there may be situations where this degree of detail is too complex for the reader, and although we want the sound of the original text, it may be better to only show the simpler key information symbols for 'Is this a dagger?' and omit the rest of the sentence. On the other hand, if the symbols are being used to cue recall of the text – say for a performance in assembly – then the symbol for 'before' may be a better choice than the symbol for 'in front'.

There are no rights and wrongs in this situation. It will require the sensitive intervention of the teacher, who will need to decide what is most important in any context.

Signs

Similar issues are involved in translating from text to sign. In a literal word-to-sign approach the words are translated in their original order, but this may result in a less direct and meaningful communication than if the meaning is put directly into sign. For example, in the following extract from *Macbeth*, the first part of the conversation translates easily into sign. However, Lady Macbeth's final words are metaphorical, and of the three possible versions, the third (c) is probably the clearest.

Original text	Possible sign versions
My dearest love Duncan comes here tonight	MY LOVE KING D COME HERE TONIGHT
And when goes hence?	WHEN GO?
Tomorrow as he purposes	TOMORROW SAME HE THINK
Oh never Shall sun that morrow see	(a) NEVER SUN DAY SEE (b) SUNRISE NEVER (c) TOMORROW NEVER

Certain principles of language should ideally be respected in word-to-sign translation. The grammar of sign dictates that you should remember where your sign for COME originated when you sign TOMORROW SAME HE THINK and make sure to sign HE in that location. This tells the viewer that it is the same person coming (Duncan) who is thinking of leaving tomorrow. In option (a), the sign for SEE should be angled down from the position of SUN towards the position of DAY, indicating that SUN is the subject of the verb and DAY is the object.

Note also that the visual logic of sign language makes it more appropriate to put NEVER at the end of the sequence rather than at the beginning, because you have to establish an entity in space before you can negate it.

Sign language also has individual formal properties, which create visual dynamic images that are important in poetry. In version (c) the BSL sign for SUN is the same as LIGHT, made at eye level. The hand opens out in a short movement down and toward the signer so that the fingers are spread and pointed. The pointed finger of the sign SEE which follows has a visual echo of SUN in its handshape. If you are going to sign a poem or story, it is a good idea to rehearse it a few times in front of a mirror so you can see what combinations of signs work best.

If you know some vocabulary but are unfamiliar with the structure of sign language, do not be too worried. As with symbols, you may choose to translate only a few key words into sign – just keep the meaning clear and comprehensible to your students. The *Dictionary of British Sign Language* is an invaluable source for sign translation. However, do not be seduced into thinking that you always have to find the exact specific sign; it may be more appropriate to use the vocabulary with which pupils are familiar. For example, although there is a BSL 'sign' for still, the refrain from 'The Strange Guest' can be signed as follows:

And still she sat, and still she reeled	SIT SPIN (outline of spinning wheel)
And still she wished for company	WANT FRIEND

In conclusion, whether you are planning to translate into sign or symbol, the most important thing to remember is to give some thought to the meaning of the text, the role of translation and the needs of your students.

3 Teaching resources

Most of the resources listed here are aimed at the mainstream, since there is still very little currently available which takes account of the needs of pupils with difficulties in language and communication. You are strongly recommended to obtain copies on sale or return and consider whether the resource is appropriate to your needs. The best resources will be ones that give you ideas and deepen your understanding of the text – giving you confidence to adapt them creatively in your own teaching.

Organisations

National Centre for Literacy and Learning (http://www.ncll.org.uk) Collection of over 18,000 trade and education publications published during the last five years. You can visit the centre or search their database for resources on-line.

Centre for Literacy in Primary Education (http://www.clpe.co.uk) Educational centre for schools and teachers, parents, teaching assistants and other educators. CLPE has a good range of publications to support the teaching of literature to primary-aged children. Core book collections are good quality texts selected for particular purposes, in consultation with teachers, with specific criteria in mind for each collection. They are detailed in *The Core Book List* published by CLPE and updated every two years. This is a good starting point for collections of poetry and stories.

Try *Book-based Reading Games* by Helen Bromley – a collection of games based on books and stories for using with primary-age pupils.

The English and Media Centre (http://www.englishandmedia.co.uk) Centre for the teaching of English and Media in secondary schools, has some of the best mainstream resources, which you will need to adapt but which will give you inspiration. Examples include: *Working with Sherlock Holmes*, KS2 English and Literacy pack; *Gulliver's Travels*.

Storytracks (http://www.storytracks.com) is an organisation which helps people of all abilities and ages to listen to stories and to start telling and sharing their own stories. The website shows projects run by Nicola Grove with adults with learning disabilities in London, and by Keith Park at the Globe Theatre with local children with severe and profound learning difficulties. There are resources to download, a list of publications and information about workshops and training. Storytrack workshops are designed for children and adults with severe communication difficulties, including: profound and multiple disabilities, learning disabilities, autistic spectrum disorders and specific language impairments.

Resources designed for pupils with special educational needs

Questions Publishing Company has one of the best lists of resources for pupils with special educational needs (http://www.questions onlinecatalogue.co.uk).

David Fulton Inclusive Readers include *The Tempest*. These could be helpful as resources to back up more dramatic and creative work with the texts.

Reading for All. A resource pack for parents and schools, produced with the support of National Year of Reading funding, that will help children and young adults with severe and profound multiple learning difficulties to make the most of stories and reading. The pack is full of ideas and practical suggestions for using stories, books, technology and libraries. All ideas in the pack were provided by parents, teachers and carers. Cost £20 (plus £2.50 p&p) for school and libraries; £10 (plus £2.50 p&p) for Mencap locations; £5 (plus £2.50 p&p) for parents. http://www.mencap.org.uk
Contact: Mencap Public Liaison Unit. Tel: 020 7696 5593.

Pupils with Special Educational Needs in the Literacy Hour. DfEE-produced free guide.
Contact: DfEE Publications on 0845 60 222 60. Reference: 0101/2000.

Reading for All. Ideas for stories and reading for children and young adults with severe and profound learning disabilities. The selection of stories ranges adapted nursery rhymes to excerpts from classical tales and includes advice on how to present them. (Mencap Year of Reading Project 1999). Available from Mencap National Centre, 123 Golden Lane, London EC1Y 0RT.

Story/Symbol Packs
Available from the Call Centre at Dundee. A set of materials to help people develop interactive reading with seven picture story books (published by Walker Books) for young children. The packs consist of the stories (*Ten in the Bed, Walking through the Jungle, Owl Babies, The Big Red Bus, The Train Ride, The Bear and the Scary Night*), symbol charts to help children choose which story they like, story topic charts

and stickers for Big Mack communication aids: www.callcentre. education.ed.ac.uk/aacresoures

Storysacks (http://www.storysack.com)
A Storysack is a large cloth bag containing a children's book with supporting materials to stimulate reading activities and make shared reading a memorable and enjoyable experience. The Storysacks project was a Basic Skills Agency National Support Project and is now run on a freelance basis by Neil Griffiths, who first conceived the idea. Contact for Storysacks: Neil Griffiths, Corner to Learn Ltd, Willow Cottage, 26 Purton Stoke, Swindon SN5 4JF. Tel/Fax: 01793 421168. Mobile: 07976 574627.

Bag Books (http://www.bagbooks.org)
Multisensory story packs for children and adults with profound learning disabilities, developed by Chris Fuller when she was teaching in a special school. The tactile stories are specially devised to suit the medium and are designed to be interactively told, with each page representing one idea, with a tactile prop. 60 Walham Grove, London SW6 1QR.

http://www.dundee.ac.uk/pamis/projects/sensory.htm
PAMIS has developed through its 'The Real Lives: Real Stories Project' over 50 personalised multi-sensory stories. The stories were adapted from Chris Fuller's Bag Books (www.bagbooks.org) approach.

Multi-sensory story-packs for children, young people and adults with learning disabilities and/or sensory impairment.

Duplicates of these stories have been made to create a library of sensory stories that can be borrowed by schools, day services and families.

http://www.symbolworld.org
Lots of stories in symbol form, on a very accessible website.

Peter. M. & Sherratt-Smith, D. (2001). *Developing Drama and Play for Children with Autistic Spectrum Disorders*. London: David Fulton The best book around for working with children on the autistic spectrum.

Books Beyond Words
Books for people who find pictures easier to understand than words, dealing with real-life issues. Pre-payment is required before any books can be sent. Contact: Book Sales, The Royal College of Psychiatrists, 17 Belgrave Square, London, SW1X 8PG. Tel: 0207 2352351 ext:146. www.rcpsych.ac.uk/publications/bbw/index.htm

Reading and Writing for Individuals with Down Syndrome, Sue Buckley. This guide provides an overview of current research and practice on how children with Down syndrome learn to read and write, providing examples of effective teaching strategies. Contact: The Down Syndrome Educational Trust, The Sarah Duffen Centre, Belmont Street,

Street, Southsea, Portsmouth PO5 1NA. Tel: 023 9282 4261.   Fax: 023 9282 4265.   Email:enquiries@downsnet.org.   Website: www.down-syndrome.info/

Specific texts

Dragonslayer by Rosemary Sutcliff. Pack of activities about the story of Beowulf, with photocopiable resources and teachers' notes. Questions Publishing, ISBN: 1-898149-52-6.

Resource packs on *The Story of Tracy Beaker* and Ann Fine's *Bill's New Frock*, popular KS2 texts. Available from Questions Publishing.

Gulliver's Travels by Carolyn Fyfe. Multisensory adaptation designed for pupils with severe and profound learning difficulties. Available from Bag Books.

Kalevala and Children of Lir. Multisensory versions of these traditional stories, one from Finland, one from Ireland. Download from http://www.storytracks.com

Sensory stories

http://www.moorcroft.hillingdon.sch.uk/sensory_stories

Taming of the Shrew
Hindu families
Canterbury Tales

Straightforward approaches to telling classic stories, backed up with music, drama and tactile illustrations. They work with simplified versions and don't suggest actual text extracts, which you need to choose yourself.

Odyssey Now, Nicola Grove and Keith Park (1996). Jessica Kingsley Publishers.
The story of the Odyssey is divided into eight episodes, told through multisensory games, artwork and music associated with different moods. The resource is designed for pupils with sensory and communication difficulties, including those with profound disabilities. A communication framework is included so that each activity can be used to develop interaction skills.

Lofty Visits The Farm is a professionally recorded production on audio CD and Story Script. combined with a Teacher's Guide (suitable for children up to age 11) – all you need to provide are the props and the actors, and you are ready to go! Full details and an audio trailer can be found at www.vocalimage.co.uk and Vocal Image can be contacted on 01483 211711 http://www.cerl.net/storysensation.htm

Sensory Drama for Very Special People. Flo Longhorn (2000) Catalyst Education ISBN 1-900231-45-X. Ideas for developing drama with children with severe and profound disabilities.

Shakespeare

Shakespeare for All series from Questions Publishing: *Romeo and Juliet, Midsummer Night's Dream, Julius Caesar.*

Much Ado About Nothing resource with photographs, film stills, cartoons and charts. Designed for KS3 pupils.

Twelfth Night Video Pack. Photocopiable pages of classroom activities, with clips from different productions of the play.
Both from the English and Media Centre.

Macbeth.
Teaching Social Cognition through Drama and Literature for People with Learning Disabilities: Macbeth in Mind. Nicola Grove and Keith Park (2001) Jessica Kingsley Publishers.
   This version of the play emphasises the ways in which characters have to work out what others are thinking and feeling, and is particularly designed for pupils with autistic spectrum disorders and problems in social relationships. After acting out a scene there are three levels of question designed for pupils at different stages of development, including those with profound disabilities.

Romeo and Juliet, Macbeth, Midsummer Night's Dream. Graphic versions designed for pupils with literacy difficulties. Available from Cutting Edge Publications, 26 Haytor Drive, Milber, Newton Abbot, South Devon TQ12 4DU.

Romeo and Juliet, Nicola Grove and Keith Park. Multisensory activities designed around the text. Available from Bag Books.

Teaching poetry

A Year with Poetry. Myra Barrs and Michael Rosen. Available from CLPE. ISBN 1-872267-12-2.
Ten teachers record their journey into teaching poetry – more particularly, into teaching poetry writing. They were guided on this journey by Michael Rosen, and by each other, throughout a year-long in-service training course during which they each kept a journal. Each chapter records not only what their children achieved with them, but also their own personal development.

Hands-on Poetry. Myra Barrs and Sue Ellis. ISBN 1 872267 076. Drawing together a broad range of ideas and activities, it includes suggestions for developing children's understanding of poetry through talk and drama, reading and writing, music and art.

Poetry Society (www.poetrysociety.org.uk)
For the last three years, the Society has produced a set of special needs resources written by Nicola Grove for the poems promoted through National Poetry Day, for both primary- and secondary-aged pupils.

The Poetry Society also produces some great resources for mainstream: posters, anthologies and the *Poetry Forager* CD-ROM, with over 800 classic poems that you can search by theme to print off, hand around, stick up on the wall, project into drama and dance installations, use as starting points for art projects.

They have a recommended list of poetry books and their own anthologies are a good source: *The Poetry Book* and *Jump Start*.

KS1 Poetry Pack, KS2 Poetry Pack available from Questions Publishing.

Me and My World, Julie Ward. Funded by the Mencap City Foundation, this is a collection of 50 poems designed for use with pupils with special educational needs. For further information, email DrNicolaGrove@aol.com

The Poetry Video available from The English and Media Centre is a collection of high quality readings of poems.

Sounds like Poetry available from David Fulton Inclusive Readers. Ideas for using sound poems linked to the National Literacy Scheme.

Puppets
Astell Burt, C. *I Am the Story: A Manual of Special Puppetry Projects* (2000) Caroline Astell Burt. Souvenir Press, ISBN 0-28563-619-7

Puppets by Post, ISBN 0-143871-40-09, www.PuppetsByPost.com

Storytelling
Bowkett, S. (2001) *What's the Story? Games and Activities for Creative Storymaking*. A&C Black.
Grugeon, E. and Gardner, P. (2000) *The Art of Storytelling for Teachers and Pupils: Using Stories to Develop Literacy in Primary Classrooms*. David Fulton.
Jennings, S. (2004) *Creative Storytelling for Children at Risk*. Speechmark, www.speechmark.net
Park, K. (2004) *Interactive Storytelling: Developing Inclusive Stories for Children and Adults*. Speechmark www.speechmark.net

Black Sheep Press produce packs associated with Becky Shanks' Narrative Approach, www.blacksheeppress.co.uk

Speaking & Listening Through Narrative
This pack is aimed at Key Stage 1 and follows the development of narrative skills in children from raising awareness of the individual

components of a simple story, to retelling and then generating their own ideas for stories.

Nursery *Narrative Pack* introduces the concepts of 'Who', 'When' and 'What happened next' within a structured yet flexible framework.

Reception Narrative Pack
The pack uses a narrative framework, raising awareness of individual components of a basic story, 'Who', 'Where', 'When', and 'What happened next', at the same time focusing on attention and listening skills, verbal understanding, and the development of spoken language.

Society for Storytelling (www.sfs.org.uk)
Provides information, resources and networking. Annual conference and brilliant website, which links you to lots of international story circles on the web.

School of Storytelling – wide range of courses throughout the year. Emerson College, Forest Row, East Sussex RH18 5JX. Tel. 01342 822238).
(www.emerson.org.uk)

There are a number of sources of information on access technology, including devices, software and learning strategies:

www.semerc.com
www.inclusive.co.uk
www.cenmac.com
www.ace-centre.org.uk
www.becta.org.uk

4 Example of story analysis

The components of narrative were listed in Chapter 6, as follows:

Structural	Emotional	Social	Rhetorical
Introductions and *closures* to the story *Orientation* (who, when, where information) *Sequences of actions* *Climax* or 'high point' of the story *Resolution:* how the story ends	*Verbal aspects:* reference to feelings, thoughts and motivations of characters *Non-verbal aspects:* stress, pausing, pitch, volume of voice, facial expression and body movement	*Ways of getting listeners to attend:* Hey, listen! *Checking and monitoring listener reactions:* (Yes? You know?) *Responding to listeners' feedback*	*Use of figurative language (metaphor and simile)* *Well-known sayings:* (Went like clockwork; You could have knocked me down with a feather) *Repetition for effect:* (first we went... then we went... then we went...) *Use of formulae and conventions:* (on and on; time and again)

When looking at a transcribed narrative, these elements can be identified line by line as in the following conversational story provided by a 12-year-old in a family discussion of holidays.

'Well, you know what?' (*Opening phrase to gain attention.*)
'It was when we were on holiday.' (*Introduction.*)

'We were on a boat on the Broads, me and my mum and dad and brother and sister' (*Orientation.*)

'And my dad was always telling us what to do, 'cos he said he was the captain and we were the crew' (*Reference to feelings and thoughts and motivation.*)

'So one day I was up the front' (*Orientation.*)

And he was steering and we were getting near the bank, and he wanted us to moor there. (*Sequence of events/actions; reference to motivation.*)

'So he shouted "Jump! Go on, jump!"' (*Stress, pitch, intonation; causal sequence.*)

'But I was looking down, and you know what?' (*Monitoring.*)

'It was really, really muddy' (*Repetition for effect.*)

'So I looked back and said "But Dad"' (*Causal sequence.*)

'And he roared at me' (*Figurative language.*)

'Jump, for goodness sake!' (*Stress, pitch, intonation.*)

'So I did. And I landed in this absolutely disgusting, smelly, black, sticky mud.' (*Descriptive language; sequence of events/actions climax of story.*)

'And I was soaking wet' (*Descriptive and emotional language.*)

'And had to change all my clothes, and they never really.' (*Emphatic language*) 'got clean again.' (*Resolution*).

'That was the funniest thing that happened on my holidays.' (*Closure and evaluation.*)

Alternative frameworks for analysing narrative can be found in McCabe and Bliss (2003).

Bibliography

Allen, A. and Coley, J. (1995) *Dance for All*. London: David Fulton.

Allen, M., Kertoy, M., Sherblom, J. and Pettit, J. (1994) Children's narrative productions: a comparison of personal event and fictional stories. *Applied Psycholinguistics*, **15**, 149–76.

Baron-Cohen, S. (1993) From attention-goal psychology to belief-desire psychology. In S. Baron-Cohen, H. Tager-Flusberg and D. Cohen (eds) *Understanding Other Minds: Perspectives from Autism*. Oxford: Oxford Medical Publications.

Bishop, D. and Edmundson, A. (1987) Language-impaired four-year-olds: distinguishing transient from persistent impairment. *Journal of Speech and Hearing Disorders*, **52**, 155–73.

Bloom, L. (1993) *The Transition from Infancy to Language: Acquiring the Power of Expression*. Cambridge: Cambridge University Press.

Brown, E. (1996) *Religious Education for All*. London: David Fulton.

Campion, C. (1997) An exploration of Cummins' theory of basic inter-personal skills and cognitive academic language proficiency, relating to bilingual children with special educational needs. MSc., University of London Institute of Education.

Coupe, J. and Goldbart, J. (1988) *Communication Before Speech*. London: David Fulton.

Crystal, D. (1997) Language play and linguistic intervention. *Child Language Teaching and Therapy*, **13**, 328–45.

DES (1989) *English for Ages 5–16* (The Cox Report). London: HMSO.

Detheridge, T. and Detheridge, M. (2002) *Literacy Through Symbols*. London: David Fulton.

Fabbretti, D., Pizzuto, E., Vicari, S. and Volterra, V. (1997) A story description task in children with Down's syndrome: lexical and morphosyntactic abilities. *Journal of Intellectual Disability Research*, **41**(2), 165–79.

Fitzpatrick, J. (1988) Literature and special needs in the primary school. T. Roberts (ed.) *Encouraging Expression Arts in the Primary Curriculum*. London: Cassell.

Fox, C. (1993) *At the Very Edge of the Forest: The Influence of Literature on Storytelling by Children*. London: Cassell.

Fyfe, C. (1996) *New Horizons*. (Unpublished).

Goldman, S. (2002) Unshared lives: fictional and personal narrative productions in high functioning autistic children. Dissertation Abstracts International, Section B: The Sciences and Engineering, 63(3-B), September, 1587, US: University Microfilms International.

Goleman, D. (1996) *Emotional Intelligence*. London: Bloomsbury Press.

Goodman, E. (1981) Aesthetic developments in the visual mode. In M. Ross (ed.) *Assessment and Education in the Arts*. Oxford: Pergamon Press, 53–75.

Gray, B. and Ridden, G. (1999) *Lifemaps of People with Learning Disabilities*. London: Jessica Kingsley.

Grove, N. (2004) Once upon a time. *Special Children*, May/June 16–19.

Grove, N. and Park, K. (1996) *Odyssey Now*. London: Jessica Kingsley.

Hardy, B. (1975) *Tellers and Listeners*. London: Athlone Press.

Hayward, D. and Schneider. P. (2000) Effectiveness of teaching story grammar knowledge to preschool children with language impairment. *Child Language Teaching & Therapy*, **16**, 255–84.

Hemphill, I., Feldman, H., Camp, I., Griffin, T., Miranda, A. and Wolf, D. (1994) Developmental changes in narrative and non-narrative discourse in children with and without brain injury. *Journal of Communication Disorders*, **27**, 107–33.

Hicks, D. (1990) Narrative skills and genre knowledge: ways of telling in the primary school grades. *Applied Psycholinguistics*, **11**, 83–104.

Howlin, P., Baren-Cohen, S. and Hadwin, J. (1999) *Teaching Children with Autism to Mindread*. Chicester: Wiley.

Keen, E. (2004) Developing the personal event narratives of children with autistic spectrum disorders. BSc Dissertation. London: City University.

Knowles, W. and Masidlover, M. (1982) *The Derbyshire Language Scheme*. Derbyshire County Council.

Labov, W. and Waletzky, J. (1967) Narrative analysis: oral versions of personal experience. In J. Helm (ed.) *Essays in the Verbal and Visual Arts*. Seattle: University of Washington Press, 12–44.

Latham, A. and Miles, A. (2001) *Communication, Curriculum and Classroom Practice*. London: David Fulton.

Locke, A. (1985) *Living Language*. Windsor: NFERNelson.

Loveland, K. and Tunali, B. (1993) Narrative language in autism and the theory of mind hypothesis: a wider perspective. In S. Baron-Cohen, H. Tager-Flusberg and D. Cohen (eds) *Understanding Other Minds: Perspectives from Autism*. Oxford: Oxford Medical Publications, 244–66.

McCabe, A. and Bliss, L. (2003) *Patterns of Narrative Discourse: A Multicultural Lifespan Approach*. Boston: Pearson Education.

McCabe, A. and Peterson, C. (eds) (1991) *Developing Narrative Structure*. Hillsdale, NJ: LEA.

Middleton, D. and Hewitt, H. (1999) Remembering as social practice: identity and life story work in transitions of care for people with profound learning disabilities. *Narrative Inquiry*, **9**, 97–121.

Milosky, L. (1987) Narratives in the classroom. *Seminars in Speech and Language,* **8**(4), 329–43.

Miranda, A., McCabe, A. and Bliss, L. (1998) Jumping around and leaving things out. *Applied Psycholinguistics,* **19**, 657–68.

Musselwhite, C. (1990) Topic setting: generic and specific strategies. In *Fourth Biennial International ISAAC Conference on Augmentative and Alternative Communication.* Stockholm.

National Curriculum Council (1992) *Curriculum Guidance 9: The National Curriculum and Pupils with Severe Learning Difficulties.* York: NCC.

Nelson, K. (1973) Structure and strategy in learning to talk. *Monographs of the Society of Research in Child Development,* **38** (serial number 149).

Nelson, K. (1986) Event knowledge and cognitive development. In K. Nelson (ed.) *Event Knowledge: Structure and Function in Development.* Hillsdale, NJ: LEA, 87–118.

Nind, M. and Hewitt, D. (1994) *Access to Communication: Developing the Basics of Communication with People with Severe Learning Difficulties.* London: David Fulton.

Norbury, C. and Bishop, D. (2003) Narrative skills of children with communication impairments. *International Journal of Language and Communication Disorders,* **38**, 287–313.

Norwich, B. (1996) Special needs education or education for all: connective specialisation or ideological impurity. *British Journal of Special Education,* **23**, 100–9.

Oakhill, J. (1994) Individual differences in children's text comprehension. In M. Gernsbacher (ed.) *The Handbook of Psycholinguistics.* San Diego, CA: Academic Press.

Paley, V. (1994) Every child a storyteller. In J. Duchan *et al.* (eds) *Pragmatics: From Theory to Practice.* New Jersey: Prentice Hall, 10–19.

Park, K. (2004) *Interactive Storytelling.* Bicester: Speechmark.

Paul, R. and Smith, R. (1993) Narrative skills in four-year-olds with typical, impaired and late-developing language. *Journal of Speech and Hearing Research,* **36**, 592–8.

Peter, M. (1994) *Drama for All.* London: David Fulton.

Peter, M. (1996) *Art for All.* London: David Fulton.

Peter, M. and Sherratt-Smith, D. (2001) *Developing Drama and Play for Children with Autistic Spectrum Disorders.* London: David Fulton.

Reilly, J., Klima, E. and Bellugi, U. (1990) Once more with feeling: affect and language in atypical populations. *Development and Psychopathology,* **2**, 367–91.

Roberts, T. (ed.) (1988) *Encouraging Expression: The Arts in the Primary Curriculum.* London: Cassell.

Ross, M. (1978) *The Creative Arts.* London: Heinemann Educational.

Roth, F. and Spekman, N. (1984) Assessing the pragmatic abilities of children. *Journal of Speech and Hearing Disorders,* **19**, 2–17.

Schneider, P. and R. Dubé (1997) Effect of pictorial versus oral story presentation on children's use of referring expressions in retell. *First Language*, 17, 283–302.

Shanks, B. (2003) Only a story? *SLT in Practice*, Spring, 10–13.

Shanks, B. and Rippon, R. (2003) *Speaking and Listening through Narrative: A Pack of Activities and Ideas.* Black Sheep Press.

Snow, C. (1983) Literacy and language: relationships during the preschool years. *Harvard Educational Review*, 53(2), 165–89.

Sperber, D. and Wilson, D. (1986) *Relevance: Communication and Cognition.* Oxford: Blackwell.

Stein, N. and Albro, E. (1997) Building complexity and coherence: children's use of goal-structured knowledge in telling stories. In M. Bamberg (ed.) *Narrative Development: Six Approaches.* NJ: LEA, 5–40.

Webb, E. (1992) *Literature in Education: Encounter and Experience.* London: Falmer Press.

Weir, R. (1962) *Narratives from the Crib.* The Hague: Mouton.

Wills, P. and Peter, M. (1995) *Music for All.* London: David Fulton.